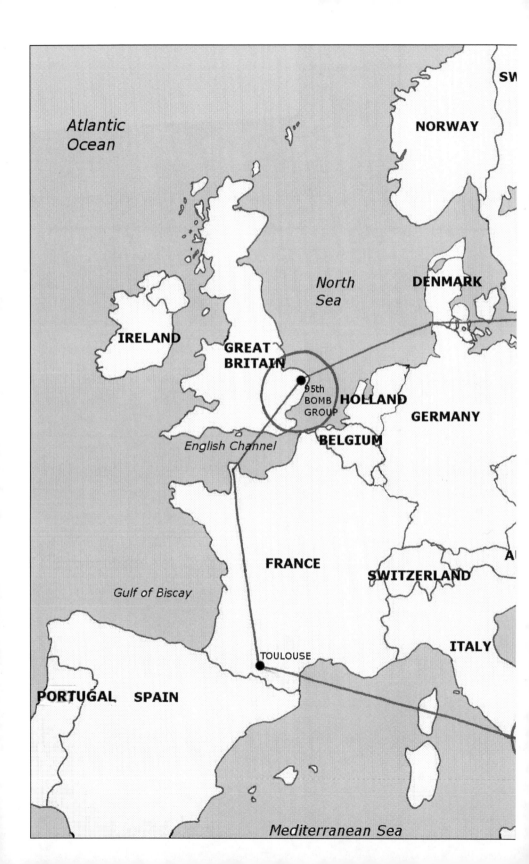

It Only Takes One

Memoirs of a Tail Gunner

1943 High School Graduation

Football

Private

By
Larry Stevens

We were told not to make notes of our missions, but everyone did it. There is more to a mission than just the takeoffs and landings. Some of my missions are sketchy and short. This book is based on my notes and memories, vague as they may be.

ISBN:1481997343
ISBN-13: 978-1481997348

ACKNOWLEDGMENTS

To my loyal princess, Stacey, my granddaughter, who found time amongst her college studies to type my manuscript and prep it for printing.

I am truly a very lucky grandfather.

Larry and Stacey

INTRODUCTION

My story is written because we survived. The truly great stories that will never be told are the ones that have been blown away by the wind, leaving the skies clean for a new day.

The skies have no memories of yesterday.

Larry Stevens

FULL HOUSE

This is the plane our ten man crew flew twenty-nine of our thirty-five combat missions in over Europe. *Full House* was a B-17 G Model with a chin turret and F model hand held tail guns.

Full House, the plane I flew in for the majority of my missions

The crew chief was M/SGT Alteri from Chicago. Alteri named the ship *Full House* because the last five digits of its ID number located on the tail were 97797, which would make a full house in poker. He also had a display of five cards as in a poker hand painted on the nose of the ship. In poker, a full house is a very good hand.

With thirty-four missions flown, we were sent to a rest home located in Black Pool, England, to await our navigator and bombardier who bailed out over Russia because of a fire located in the transfer valves under our top turret.

A new crew on their first mission flew our plane and was shot down over the target and took down another B-17 with them—**IT ONLY TAKES ONE.**

IT ONLY TAKES ONE

- That's for me!

- Be careful what you ask for.

- **IT ONLY TAKES ONE.**

I have thirty-five combat missions over enemy occupied Europe as a tail gunner on B-17s. I have the air medal with five Oak Leaf Clusters and a DFC (Distinguished Flying Cross). I also have a medal given to me by the Russian Government. I am not a hero. I am one of the lucky ones that finished a tour of duty and came back alive.

It has been said:

"If you want to meet a hero, go to the cemetery."

Like anyone that has experienced combat of any sort, I have a story.

My family- (Left to Right) Dad, Mom, Ernie, Mayme, Jim, Me and Mary Lou

MY EARLY YEARS, PRIOR TO THE WAR

I was born on July 10, 1924 in the city of Alhambra, California, in my parents' home just seven miles from downtown Los Angeles City Hall.

My grammar school friend, Chuck Titus, was also born in Alhambra. His father said, "Best location in the world. If you work in L.A., the sun is at your back in the a.m. going to work. When you return home at quitting time, the sun is still at your back."

In the 1920s and 1930s, Alhambra was considered to be a small country town. We had meadowlarks, open land, horses and skies so blue they were near to purple. No smog. The mountains seemed so near you could touch them. Atlantic Boulevard, the main street of Alhambra, was dirt and peppertree lined. Prior to being called Atlantic Boulevard, it was called "Wilson Boulevard" since it was the road leading to Mount Wilson Observatory.

The 1930s was an era where no doors were locked and people helped each other. It was an era of comics in the newspaper that were funny. The days of Wimpy saying "I'll gladly pay you Tuesday for a hamburger today." Of Kickapoo Joy Juice, Popeye and Olive Oyl, Katz and Jammer and the little guy, Hitch Hiker, dressed in an overcoat with the collar turned up and a cloud raining over his head saying, "Nov Shmoz Ka Pop."

My family was made up of three boys and two girls, a total of five of us besides Mom and Dad (Belle (Valenzuela) Stevens and Tony Stevens). Ernie was the oldest, then Mayme, Jimmy, Me and the youngest, Mary Lou. I know I was born in heaven because I could not have asked for a better mom and dad. My two brothers and two sisters were also the best any son or brother could wish for.

2

MOM AND DAD

Mom and Dad – around 1938

Dad was born in Santa Barbara, California in 1895. Mom was born in Madera, California in 1900.

The Depression came in 1929, and it was terribly hard on the grown folks. Everyone struggled to put food on the table. I well recall my mother taking me in our car to a bank on West Main Street in Alhambra in the 1930s. The bank was closed and boarded up. On either side of the bank were vacant lots and weeds. I remember my mother saying as she got out of the car, "We've got money in this bank. If I can just get a janitor to give us $5.00, we can make out for a month." She knocked on every boarded up door and window of the bank, to no avail.

The 1930s were truly hard times, but for some reason, we kids never seemed to want. Mom always had food on our table and clean clothes for us.

My father, a plaster contractor, poured endless hours into eking out a living for us and the crew of men who worked for him.

He would rise at 4:00 a.m., yet I am not so sure he would ever go to bed. I know he figured plans until the wee hours every morning. When we kids were sick, he and Mom were there all night for us and they were equally as sick.

Dad's highest success in school was the 4th grade. He never gave himself credit for the wonderful person he was, he just worked hard to achieve.

One last story about Dad. In the summer of 1938, when I started my plastering career, Dad would get us workers squared away and out onto the job. He would then put on his only suit of clothes and only pair of shoes and go out and figure jobs. At noon, he would come onto the job and sit

3

with us workers. He never carried a sack lunch as the others of us did, so all of the fellows would offer him a tidbit of theirs. One evening, I asked him why he did not carry a lunch like the other fellows. Dad said, "The fellows had very little to offer, but when they offered to share with me, the boss, it made them feel very proud." Dad only went to the fourth grade in school, but he sure understood people. Dad never pushed his men. After lunch, dad would take off his suit coat, roll up his sleeves, grab a hawk and trowel and work with the fellows for an hour. Dad was called the "Boss," but he was just one of the guys. We all admired him.

If Dad was up at 4:30 a.m., so was Mom. She had clothes that needed to be washed (I remember her scrub board), ironing to be done and clothes to be mended, especially socks. By 6:00 a.m., Mom would get us up. If it was winter, she would carry us little ones into the living room where we had our only gas heater. She would dress us there while we shivered. Our breakfast was oatmeal or cold cereal. One time, one of my friends did not come to school, so the following day I asked how he got away with it. "It was easy," he said, "I just told my mom I didn't feel good, so she let me stay home."

The next morning, I walked into the kitchen while Mom was ironing. I announced, "I am not going to school because I have a stomachache." All the while I was tearing open a box of shredded wheat with my finger, which I cut on the top tape. I almost cried as I showed my mother my bleeding finger. She said, "God punished you, there is an open box of Post Toasties® there on the table." At about ten minutes to 8:00 a.m., Mom took me by the arm, handed me my sack lunch, gave me a light swat on my butt and said, "Leave now or you're going to be late." I cried all the way to school, but from kindergarten to eighth grade, I had perfect attendance.

ERNIE

My brother, Ernie, in the late 1930s

4

My eldest brother, Ernie Stevens was born on September 28, 1918.

In 1933, the city of Long Beach suffered a severe earthquake. Mom sent me to get my brother Ernie for dinner. He was selling newspapers at our local grocery store, Torlies. He stacked the last few papers he had not sold and placed a rock and a can on them. He trusted people would be honest. It was a tough era for money, but to my knowledge, very few people cheated.

As we walked home, my brother looked up at the telephone wires and started to run. He said, "Come on, Jeepers." I needed no encouragement. I ran scared but did not know why.

I recall racing through the empty lot and watching my brother's feet part the green grass. As we entered the house, everyone was sitting at our dining room table. The chandelier was swinging back and forth and the teacups were flipping on the saucers. We had no carpeting and our piano rolled from one wall of the room to the other. The quake seemed to last three to five minutes. No one said a word.

A few days later, our dad took us to Long Beach to view the devastation of the epicenter.

Long Beach Polytechnic High School had a big ball over the patio that had dislodged and fallen. That would have been one hell of a big catch.

I also remember a hat lying in the middle of a lawn where the owner did not stop to retrieve it. Everywhere was destruction.

Ernie was like a second father to us kids. In his youth, he made model airplanes out of balsa wood and paper. He was so neat. He always won first place ribbons for his efforts. He was patient with all of us.

Ernie smoked a pipe. One day he left it on the piano, the bowl had a buildup of residue around the edges, so I was determined to clean his pipe for him. I scraped out the bowl with my pocketknife and washed the pipe with soap so that it sparkled like new. I returned the pipe to the piano. When he got home from work, he picked up the pipe and asked, "Who would do this for me?" I proudly said, "I did." He said, "The pipe residue makes a pipe sweet, but there will never be a pipe sweeter than this."

In 1941, Ernie, was inducted into the infantry at Camp Roberts, California, out of Paso Robles, about halfway up the coast from Los Angeles to San Francisco. While I was in Gunnery School in Fort Meyers, Florida in 1943, Ernie was killed while spear heading an infantry drive in Messina, Italy.

MAYME

My sister, Mayme, with Ernie in the 1940s

My sister, Mayme Stevens, was born on December 8, 1920. We have all determined she was a saint.

In the 1930s, my very good grammar school friend, Godfrey and I loved to hike the Garvey Hills, also known as Elephant Hills, due to an elephant escaping from a circus. The area is now known as Coyote Pass. Godfrey and I would catch pollywogs and frogs and bring them home to our fishpond. One day, I came home late for dinner. Everyone was seated and eating so my dad told me to go to bed without dinner. I cried and went to bed. Pretty soon, here comes my sister, Mayme, with a tray of food. I know she and Dad fixed it for me. Dad did not have a mean bone in his body, but he did have rules: always come to the table with a shirt on and be on time for dinner.

JIMMY

My brother, Jim, when entering the Merchant Marines in the early 1940s

Third in the family is my brother, Jim Stevens. He was born on November 14, 1922.

One month every summer of the 1930s, our family would go to Bakersfield and spend the entire month camping on the Kern River. We camped, swam, fished, played softball in the water, pitched horse shoes, hunted bull frogs and rabbits, and basked in the sun.

On one of our family trips to the Kern River, Jim and I were following an older neighbor that my parents had invited. The canyon walls were steep and wooded so that we all had to go into the water to get around some big rocks. Jim slipped and was swept into the rapids and went past me, waving his arms and yelling, "HELP!!"

I raced back past many rocks and arrived in camp to see Dad bringing in Jimmy under his arm with my brother Ernie swimming in beside him. My dad then laid Jim over a barrel. I was terrified, then later relieved. Jim lay over a barrel for a long time and drained a great deal of water out of his lungs. I later told my dad, "Dad, you're a hero." He said, "No, I'm not a hero. I just did what I had to do."

Another time at the river when Jim was a boy scout of 12 or 13 years and I was 10 or 11, Jim said to me, "Let's go for a walk away from the river." As we walked, Jim said, "You know, one day, water will be expensive. If you had a dollar and you were in the desert thirsting, wouldn't you pay that dollar for a glass of water?"

I do not know if this was in the same month span he had just had his fill of river water, but I have never forgotten his foresight. He also pointed out the North Star, Orion and the Big and Small Dippers. Jim was a boy scout and learned things through scouting. I knew one day I would be a boy scout.

At Marguerita Grammar School, Jimmy always met the janitor at the front door of school at 6:00 a.m. Jimmy was always the first student to arrive and he would put up the flag. In high school, Jim played "B" basketball and, even though he was small, he played varsity football. I am sure he was never more than 135 pounds. He excelled in both. In his junior year, he wrote the high school sports page and received an award from the Southern California Helms Foundation, founded by Helms Bakery. They gave him a plaque or Olympic type medallion for writing the best high school sports page. His senior year, he was the high school paper "Editor of the Year" and, again, received a Helms Foundation plaque. He was also student body president of Alhambra High School his senior year, 1941. I think he walked on water. Everybody loved Jim, especially our family.

After graduating from Alhambra High School, Jimmy went to live in Alaska. In the months after Japan bombed Pearl Harbor, he related stories about the airplanes that guarded Alaska. One story he told was about a very slow Catalina seaplane that radioed into a dispatcher, "I'm surrounded by five Japanese zeros, and I'm attacking." He was never heard from again.

When Jimmy returned home he joined the Merchant Marines. He had many harrowing stories of heads bobbing in the ocean from sunken ships and of being on a mast trying to loosen a stuck rope on a pulley with the mast swaying from side to side. Jimmy was at the helm for two hours at a time trying to head the ship into the wind during a storm while being pushed onto shore and not being able to get back on course in high winds. After a two hour break, he returned and took over the helm and immediately swung the ship around, getting it closer to the correct path. Then doing it again and again. The person he relieved said to the Captain, "This guy's crazy. Look at what he's doing." The Captain said, "He's the first one to make sense." Jimmy steered the boat straight-ahead, on the course they needed to follow. Everyone was saved.

In the letters my brother would share with the family, Jimmy told us how cold it was to stand watch aboard ship. So, when I was issued my fleece-lined flying jacket at gunnery school in Fort Meyers, Florida in 1943, I bundled it up and mailed it home to him. The next time he was at sea, he was offered $300 cash for it. Three hundred dollars then was like $3,000 now. I asked him why he did not sell it. He said, "Being warm was worth more than money." I paid charges for a new jacket and was never questioned. I took a chance on government issued clothes, but I knew he was worth it.

MARY LOU

My sister, Mary Lou in the 1940s

My youngest sister, Mary Lou Stevens, was born on September 9, 1926. Mary Lou always had time to boost my ego. I might also add, she always saw to it that I got Cheezits®'s for my birthday. That does make her special.

Jimmy and I used to share a room next to Mary Lou's room. Often times, in her sleep, Mary Lou would move around and shout in response to her dreams. One night, she woke herself up, yelling, "Help." She said she listened for someone to come in and check on her as we often did. No one came so she pulled the covers over her head and went back to sleep. The next morning, she asked, "How come you didn't check on me when I hollered, 'Help,' last night?" I responded to her, "Well, I had just come in two minutes before and you were fine!"

As kids, we rarely ever fought. The only time I can ever recall fighting was over who would do the washing of the dishes and who would do the drying of the dishes. Ernie would come in and ask what was the matter. He would ask Mary Lou what she wanted to do and he would make me do the opposite. We had a fun time growing up and we all got along.

ME

Me in the late 1930s

When we traveled to Bakersfield on the ridge route, we encountered Burma Shave signs, which I am sure helped us to learn to read.

There were six hundred jingles, which originated in 1925. The last signs were taken down in 1963.

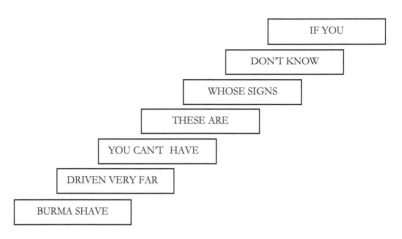

IF YOU

DON'T KNOW

WHOSE SIGNS

THESE ARE

YOU CAN'T HAVE

DRIVEN VERY FAR

BURMA SHAVE

In 1933, we elected a new president – Franklin Delano Roosevelt. I remember waking up to the song, "Happy Days Are Here Again" and hearing, "A chicken in every pot."

Very few people were working except for government employees, policemen, firemen, railroad workers, WPA (Works Progress Administration), and CCC (Civilian Conservation Corps). The sound of people working was not heard, and money was scarce. People had to share and work together. By 1939, England went to war with Germany, and wartime economy took over; that is airplanes, ships, tanks and ammunition were being built for the war. Secretly, America started a lend lease to England and Russia. Work was starting to happen. We were slowly coming out of the Depression.

I entered high school in 1939, the ninth grade. I was an average student but figured I could make a name for myself in sports. I went out for "B" football. The coach had four teams and said he was in need of a center on our single wing team. This meant I had to center the ball, not hand it off.

In our first practice, coach had me center a ball to our fullback for a sneak play that ran past me. As I centered the ball and made my block, I hit the fullback in the chest with a hard center pass. The ball bounced over the line of scrimmage for a fumble but I got a clean block and opened a nice hole for him to run through. Too bad he did not have a ball to carry. By the end of practice, the coach promoted me. I was now the entire fifth string.

My sophomore year, I was moved up to varsity as third string center and gained experience. At the end of the season, both first-string and second-string centers graduated and I moved into the first-string starting position for my junior and senior years. My senior year, I became captain of our team and we had a decent season. We won our league. We played Redondo Beach for the CIF (California Interscholastic Federation)

Championship, and we led the first three quarters of the game.

Starting the fourth quarter, we punted to the one-foot line of Redondo Beach. To play it safe, they punted back to our fifty yard line.

At this point of the game – for some unknown reason – our coach changed our outside half to the inside half (blocking back position) who played either off my right leg or left leg, depending on right formation or left formation unbalanced line. The outside half was not familiar with the inside half position.

Our quarterback called for left formation. On lining up for the play, the halfback straddled my legs. As the play began and I started to center the ball, I saw I had a leg obstruction, so I accounted for the leg and moved the ball to avoid his leg. As I made my move, his first step coincided with my move. I centered the ball and it hit the halfback's right knee. The ball bounced up and over our line of scrimmage by at least twenty feet, shades of my first year. Redondo recovered the fumble and it was their ball game after that. They became ignited and took the ball in for a score and tied the game, 14 to 14.

They had a good kick off and stopped us at about our twenty-five yard line. Our punter got off a bad punt of about five yards. They were unstoppable and the final score was 21 to 14. We lost.

The Japanese bombed Pearl Harbor, Hawaii, on December 7, 1941. I did not have a clue where Hawaii was located. By then I was sixteen and a junior in high school. I was made a block warden of our area, with Fremont Grammar School as our headquarters. This required me to notify houses in the area if there was an attack or enemy sightings.

In 1942, a Japanese submarine shelled the coast of Santa Barbara around midnight. I woke up and could hear and see the flashes of artillery shells in the sky. I figured we were being invaded. I got dressed and ran all the way to Fremont Grammar School – about three miles from our house. I only stopped long enough to advise a man in a house with all the lights on to please douse the lights. There was an air raid in progress. He said, "I know. I'm the head air raid warden of this district."

One of my very fine acquaintances, Bernie Labb, told me recently, long after the war, that he was on guard duty in San Pedro, California and witnessed a Japanese submarine raise up in the harbor and sink a freighter. He went to his supervisor and told him what he saw. His supervisor replied, "That's impossible."

Bernie and I have played many years of summer and winter basketball, including Olympic Seniors basketball for those of us over seventy years. For our Olympic Seniors basketball team, I was the youngest at 73 years of age. We won third place and received a beautiful medallion for our efforts. Perhaps you guessed it: there were only three teams in our senior league.

Bernie and I are still good friends even now in our later years of life.

We meet for lunch every third Wednesday of the month with other long time acquaintances.

The ID card I carried that identify me as a block warden

R. H. French, representing the Victory House, addressed selectees leaving from Local Board 205 this morning, and other talks were given by Jesse Ellico, president of the chamber of commerce, and Mayor Charles Varney. Rev. C. E. Britton of the Alhambra Ministerial Association also spoke. Testaments were presented the men by M. E. Scholfield of the Gideon Society.

Selectees who left for the reception center in charge of Acting Corp. Cecil Kenneth Knight, are:

Donald Reniers, 1695 Las Flores, San Marino.

William Francis Bartling, 117 South Raymond Avenue.

Howard William Von Berg, 800 Westboro Drive.

Edward Truman Sears, Gardena Hotel, Gardena.

Cecil Kenneth Knight, 1820 South Ethel Avenue.

Reginald Nelson Nickerson, 1516 Maple Street, South Pasadena.

Werner John Schram, 1206 South Palm Avenue.

John William Brockmeier, 1970 Fletcher Avenue, South Pasadena.

William Kemp Porter, 51 Hampden Terrace.

Kenneth D. Hed, 2314 Larch Street.

Paul Leonard Riccio, 1110 East Green Street, Pasadena.

Leon Edward Foley, 1821 West Commonwealth Avenue.

Jack Frederick King, 905 South Atlantic Boulevard.

Lawrence Romeo Stevens, 1102 South Edith Avenue.

Franklyn Keith Veir, 1001 Stratford Avenue, South Pasadena.

Robert Donovan Smith, 1036 Brent Avenue, South Pasadena.

Henry Veir McNulty, 1804 Alhambra Road, South Pasadena.

Robert Warren Goodknight, 1704 West Ramona Boulevard.

Robert Ivan Boone, 114 South Olive Avenue.

Kenneth Alvin Luckinbill, 2728 South Willard, San Gabriel.

Richard Charles Schattinger, 465 Plymouth Road, San Marino.

Raymond Victor Petersen, 1204 Marengo Avenue, South Pasadena.

Walter Burton Houtz, 930 North Des Robles Place.

An article from the *Alhambra Post-Advocate* on April 17, 1943

INDUCTION INTO THE U.S. ARMY 1943

All of my close high school friends graduated in February of 1943 and were immediately drafted into the service. Only two were left, Bob Boone and Bob Goodknight. They were being inducted April 10, 1943. I skipped school that day and went with them to the induction center in downtown Los Angeles to enlist. We were given a physical and accepted into the service of our country, the United States Army. We were given thirty days to take care of our business, then report for duty May 10, 1943. I was still in school, my senior year at Alhambra High School. When I returned to school, I asked my teachers if I could accelerate my classes to graduate in June with my regular class. They asked me to turn in a given amount of work, which I did. I received my diploma with my June graduating class.

On May 10, 1943, we boarded a bus in Los Angeles and were sent to a staging area in Arlington, California, about twenty-five miles east of Los Angeles. Here, we were issued uniforms and bedding. The next day, they took us to the dispensary for shots. I was injected at least three times in each arm. As I stepped out the door, one fellow took me by the arm and said, "You look pale. Better sit on this log and put your head between your legs."

At a later date, I was given an IQ test and asked what part of the Army would be of interest. I told the person, "The Air Corps through photography." That was what I had studied in school. I was given an oral examination of twelve questions about photography. I answered all twelve questions correctly.

The next thing I knew, I was in a private car on a train with eleven other fellows. We were bound for Atlantic City, New Jersey, for basic training. On the train ride to New Jersey, I met my very good friend, Harlan "Jim" Blake. He was from Pasadena, California and he was the sports editor for his high school newspaper. I was lucky he took a liking to me and we developed a very close relationship.

A drawing from my friend, Jim Blake given to me in basic training

BASIC TRAINING – ATLANTIC CITY, NEW JERSEY
THAT'S FOR ME!

Our quarters were in the Claridge Hotel, on the fourteenth story. We were on the waterfront of the Atlantic Ocean, which was approximately three-hundred yards from the beach with only the boardwalk between us. One NCO (Non Commissioned Officer) was assigned to every floor of the hotel to harass us new recruits. Our NCO was from the south and had a vocabulary of about twenty words – all curse words that he used to put a sentence together. Our working hours, from 4:00 a.m. to 11:00 p.m., were total harassment. One night, after going to bed at 11:00 p.m., all the lights went on at 11:30 p.m. and we jumped to attention in the hall. Our NCO stormed down the middle of our quarters and was berating us because someone threw a roll of toilet paper from the fourteenth floor. He said, "You know, fellows, that's a lot of shit!!" He stopped, repeated himself and said, "That's a good one. I've got to tell my friends." I believe that was the only time I ever saw him smile.

Every day but Sunday, we marched thirteen miles through the streets of Atlantic City to a city dump called Brigantine Field. As we marched, we sang air corps songs and many other tunes. We were almost like a glee club and it made marching fun. Brigantine Field was dusty from cinder ash which we stirred up with our feet. At Brigantine, we learned close order drills and how to shoot a rifle and pistol. We also ate a lot of dust.

Kitchen patrol (KP) and details such as filling gunnery sacks of sand at the rifle range were always something you had to beware of. That was extra duty. Jim and I were caught a couple of times after marching all day. They would catch us after chow hiding behind the exit doors as we were leaving. Jim and I finally got smart and exited the same way we entered.

One Sunday morning, Jim and I lingered in our room 'til about 8:00 a.m. Normally all of us fled the hotel as early as possible to avoid getting caught for extra duties.

Two NCOs entered our floor talking loud and looking for KP detail. Jim said to me, "Quick, jump into this barracks bag." He hung me over the end of our bunk beds. He then went to the bathroom, opened the curtain to the shower and placed a towel over the mirror of the medicine cabinet so it would not show him behind the door. The NCO came in, gave a cursory look, and said, "No one here." As he walked out, Jim came from behind the door and took me down from the end of the bunk. We grabbed our towels and bathing suits and went out the door. The two NCOs were right on our heels saying, "Stop! We know who you are!" We jumped every set of stairs from the fourteenth story to the bottom of the hotel where we left laughing and half-crying. We were so exhilarated. They did not catch us.

One day while marching on the boardwalk, we were halted and put "at ease." One of my buddies in rank poked me and said, "Look at the buck sergeant with the wings." He said, "That's for me." I said, "He's got wings. So that means he's a pilot." My buddy said, "Those are not pilot wings. Those are gunner's wings. I'm not going to be a pilot, that's what I want to be, a gunner." I thought to myself, "Me too. That's for me!!"

Shortly after that encounter, we were escorted to another hotel and given dexterity tests. That is to say, they gave us nuts and bolts of different sizes and we had to match them together in a given period of time. I made the time period and was taken to an interrogator. He asked me if I would like to be a gunner on airplanes. I answered, "That's for me!!"

We marched back to the Claridge Hotel, and, there, in the big glaring headlines on the news rack was, "Sixty B-17s Lost Over Schweinfurt and Regensburg." I said to myself, "That's not for me!!" The date was August 15, 1943.

A few days later, Jim and I were marching on the boardwalk again when we were halted and put at ease. We were in rank with the tallest first, four abreast. Since Jim and I were the same size and weight, we were side by side toward the front of the rank. Jim said to me, "Quick Larry. Grab me. Everything is going black." He passed out. I hollered to our drillmaster (DM), "Something's wrong with Jim."

Medics were called and Jim was taken to the hospital. At the day's end, I gathered up Jim's toilet articles and took out for the hospital. I went to the front desk and asked for Jim and the girl said, "He's in isolation. No one can visit him. He has spinal meningitis."

It must have been Saturday when this happened because I went back the next day and he was no longer isolated, so I got to visit him. At the same time Jim was stricken sick, his mother, Madge Blake, in Pasadena, California was ironing. She told me (at a later time) she got the strangest feeling something was wrong with her Jim. She said, "I immediately got to my knees and prayed to God to take care of my Jim." Then she felt the greatest feeling of calmness, like God had touched her. She knew then Jim was taken care of and that he would be okay. At that point, with Jim still in the hospital, we ended our basic training and were given orders to move.

As we were standing in ranks with bags packed in front of the hotel, Jim was released from the hospital. He came around the corner on the boardwalk and dropped everything he was carrying. He said, "You're leaving? You can't go without me." It was a tough situation, but our orders were cut and we were leaving for the train station to Armament School in Denver, Colorado. Jim stayed another few weeks and helped clean up the hotel for the returning wounded that had been hospitalized. Eventually, they sent him to Radio School in Wisconsin. We continued to stay in touch but did not see one another until after the war.

Me, Blake, Becker and Nelson

Nelson and Me

Blake and Me

Becker and Me

Me and Blake

Me and Blake

Me and Becker in Atlantic City, New Jersey with
the Claridge Hotel in the background

An article from the *Alhambra Post-Advocate*

ARMAMENT SCHOOL -- DENVER, COLORADO

From Basic Training in Atlantic City, New Jersey to Armament School in Denver, Colorado, a number of us stayed together, though some were split away to radio school, mechanical school, etc. I remember little about Armament School, except we were taught to field strip a fifty caliber machine gun blindfolded, with gloves on, and then put it back together again. We also learned about bomb racks, handguns and basics of electricity and aircraft recognition.

My most favorite memory was that I carried and chewed Chicklet gum. Every day, one fellow would come up and ask for a Chicklet. After two weeks of the same routine, I decided he needed a lesson. I put two pieces of Feen-A-Mint® laxative gum into the top of my Chicklet box and, when he came mooching, I gave him those two. A few minutes passed then his eyes opened wide and he looked at me and said, "You son of a bitch! You son of a bitch!!" as he ran out the door holding both cheeks. He never asked for another Chicklet.

BROTHERS IN SERVICE

JAMES STEVENS (left) and LAWRENCE STEVENS, sons of Mr. and Mrs. Tony Stevens, 1102 South Edith Avenue, are serving in the Merchant Marines and Army Air Corps, respectively. James, 21, is spending a leave with his parents while awaiting further sailing orders. He returned November 1 from six months active duty in the Pacific. He was commissioner general in 1940-41 at Alhambra High School, was named sports editor of the year by Helms in 1940, played varsity football and was acting captain of the B and varsity football teams. Lawrence, 19, a sergeant, is based at Fort Myers, Atlanta. In April, he was graduated from gunnery school at Florida. A graduate of Alhambra High School, he was captain of the football team and played center on the varsity football team in his senior year. Their older brother, Ernest Stevens, in the Army, was reported killed in action somewhere in Italy last month.

An article from the *Alhambra Post-Advocate*

GUNNERY SCHOOL -- FORT MEYERS, FLORIDA

When we entered gunnery school, five of us from basic training and Armament School formed a close bond. We studied together every spare moment we had through the leadership of one person, Seibold. Seibold graduated number one in our gunnery class and was so honored. Where that put the other four of us, they never told us, but of 150 questions given, Seibold answered 145 correctly. The rest of us answered 144, 143, 142 and 141. I came out in the middle with 143 correct. There was a bit of a scandal because someone had stolen the test. They called Seibold in, but there was no doubt of his honesty and ability. We all came out clean.

Besides our aircraft recognition and more armament schooling, we shot skeet once in the morning and once in the afternoon. It was like a resort. Every afternoon at about 4:00 p.m., a cloud would come over and drench us with rain, almost like a cloudburst. Big pools of water would form on the ground, but in a short time they would dry and all would become normal again.

While there in school, Mom wrote me a letter saying my brother Ernie was killed in action in Messina, Italy. He was leading a point of invasion and was shot by the enemy.

Ernie again showed his dedication to his friends by staying with them when he had his opportunity to stay out of harm's way. Prior to the invasion, where he was killed, the officer in charge asked for a volunteer who could type and was needed in the orderly room. Ernie volunteered for the position, but when his buddies were getting ready to move out, Ernie told the officer he was going with them. Ernie was a buck sergeant at the time. The officer in charge said, "If you go, you lose your stripes." Ernie would not let his friends down, and so he lost his stripes and his life.

His very good buddy, "Roddy," whom he met at Camp Roberts and entertained at our house said, "I talked to him until he died." The world lost a wonderful person and our family lost a wonderful son and brother!! At that time, I had a choice of going home for a short furlough or graduating with my gunnery school class. I chose to graduate.

Gunnery School
Fort Myers, Florida

From Left to Right:
Szoke, Me, Seibold

From Left to Right:
Szoke, Me, Seibold

Full House Crew

Top Row (From left): Navigator Morrison, Bombardier Sherwood,
Pilot Dancison, Copilot Albert "Ruby" Keeler.
Bottom Row: Waist Gunner Langford, Ball Turret Gunner Makelky, Tail Gunner
Stevens (Me), Waist Gunner Rogers, Radio Operator Comeau,
Top Turret Gunner Rich

DECEMBER 1943 – MARCH 1944

Our crew get-together for training was at Avon Park, Florida. There, we were assigned to a ten-man crew of four officers and six enlisted men.

Pilot	George Dancison	2nd LT
Copilot	Albert "Ruby" Keeler	2nd LT
Navigator	Frank Morrison	2nd LT
Bombardier	Foster Sherwood	2nd LT
Engineer	Ray Rich	SGT
Radio Op	Alyre Comeau	SGT
Ball Turret Gunner	Leo Makelky	SGT
R Waist Gunner	Gordon Langford	SGT
L Waist Gunner	Bob Rogers	SGT
Tail Gunner	Larry Stevens	SGT

In training, we enlisted men did not have any specific duties on the plane, except to share our positions and learn to live together. I practiced the duties of the radio operator and ended up taking over once when our radio operator was sick. I had to change full banks of radio frequencies and was lucky enough to get the changes right, but I sure sweated it all out.

I had also asked about our Morse code key. My radio operator said, "Don't worry about it. We don't use that key anymore." Naturally, I felt I had to practice sending out SOSs. When we landed, I heard everyone asking if they had heard the SOSs. I kept my mouth shut, but asked our Radio Operator if the key was hooked up. He said, "Yes, but it was no longer used."

I was originally assigned a waist position in the middle, or "waist," of the plane, but spent all my time in the tail. I took a dictionary with me and read from the first page to the last. Everyone laughed at me, but I did learn words like "REPARTEE," which was a quick ready reply. If I had been asked or given a chance to name our ship, "REPARTEE" was my choice. I was not asked.

On the day I acted as radio operator, we were coming in for a landing when our pilot hit prop wash, which is unstable air hurled backward from the propellers of other aircrafts. Our left wing dropped, and our pilot hit engines one and two. Immediately, we flipped the other way but, without a delay, our pilot hit engines three and four, stabilizing the ship. Talk about fast reactions. Everyone on the ground that witnessed the event was betting both wings touched the ground. I imagine we would have done a beautiful cartwheel. **IT ONLY TAKES ONE**.

Another day, I was standing in the waist of our "F" model B-17 with open side windows. It dawned on me we were a long time on takeoff. I looked forward out the side window and saw that the end of the runway was very near and there were spiked trees haphazardly awaiting us. All of a sudden, the plane rose like a fighter plane takeoff and I immediately sank to my knees. After landing, I asked the copilot, Ruby, what had happened. He said the pilot, Danny, told him to take over, but he was looking out his window and with the roar of the engines, did not hear him. At that moment, both Danny and Ruby realized no one was flying the plane and they both grabbed the wheel and pulled us in the air just missing disaster. **IT ONLY TAKES ONE**.

When crew training was over, we packed up and were sent by train to Fort Dix, New York, our port of embarkation. On Friday, March 31, 1944, we boarded the HMS Queen Elizabeth for a five day voyage to England. I wanted to see the Statue of Liberty, but after being up for forty-eight hours, I was exhausted. I found my bunk and fell fast asleep. I did not wake up until far out at sea.

Later, I found my copilot, Ruby, and he pointed out some top officials of our country- Stimson, Secretary of War, Stetinius and Tedder. He also pointed out Joe Louis, the heavy weight-boxing champion of the world.

I watched our wake and we sure kept changing directions to avoid submarines. As big as the Queen Elizabeth was, she never stopped swaying. There was a lot of seasickness, but I survived without getting sick. We landed in Scotland and were entertained by the Scottish bagpipes. No paid vacation could equal what we were experiencing. From Scotland, we were sent on to our base by train, and then by Army 4 x 4 trucks. Our base was located in the town of Horham, England.

Pilot George Dancison

Copilot Albert "Ruby" Keeler

Navigator Frank Morrison

Bombardier Foster Sherwood

Engineer / Top Turret Gunner Ray Rich

Radio Operator Alyre Comeau

Ball Turret Gunner Leo Makelky

Waist Gunner Gordon Langford

Waist Gunner Bob Rogers

Tail Gunner Larry Stevens (me)

Full House Crew: (from the left) Rogers, Makelky, Rich, Comeau, and Me

Rich, Langford, Me, Comeau,
Makelky, Rogers

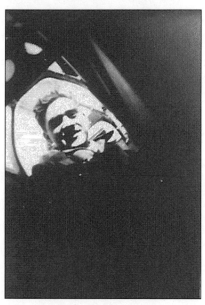

Me in the tail position

9 of the 10 *Full House* Crew:
Top Row from left: Pilot Dancison, Navigator Morrison, Waist Gunner Rogers,
Bombardier Sherwood, Tail Gunner Stevens (Me).
Bottom Row from left: Copilot Albert "Ruby" Keeler, Radio Operator Comeau,
Top Turret Gunner Rich, Ball Turret Gunner Makelky

ENGLAND

In England, the 8th Air Force consisted of 3 divisions of heavy bombers:

> 1st Division-15 groups of B-17s (Triangle Tail Marking)
> 2nd Division-15 groups of B-24s
> 3rd Division-15 groups of B-17s (Square Tail Marking)

The total was 45 heavy bomber bases in England. The second division was later sent to Italy, I believe in July of 1944, because the B-24s could travel further and faster than our B-17s.

Each bomber group had four squadrons. Each squadron housed seven to twelve airplanes, depending on what Uncle Sam could deliver. At least five or six airplanes had to be flyable from each squadron. With four squadrons of five each, a group could put twenty airplanes with one or two extras to fill in for any planes that might abort.

Three groups of twenty airplanes each or sixty in all was called a wing. In our case, our wing was composed of the 95th Bomb Group, B the 100th Bomb Group, D and the 390th Bomb Group, J . The letters of each group were painted in a large square on our tail for ID.

Each ship carried thirteen guns so, with sixty ships flying a tight formation, we formed a very formidable defense unit.

On Tuesday, April 11, 1944, at 8:15 p.m., our ten-man crew arrived at our new home base in Horham, England, the 95th Bomb Group of B-17s. On the ship's tail of the B-17 was painted a big square "B," which in the air identified us as the 95th Bomb Group. We were assigned to the 412th bomb squadron and sent to the orderly room to get our living quarters assigned to us.

On the counter of the orderly room were forty wallets. I asked, "What are the forty wallets?" The orderly answered, "You're their replacements. We lost four crews yesterday. Welcome to the real world!" I am not sure the orderly understood. I was there to become a hero, not get myself killed. After receiving our bedding, we were shown to our sleeping quarters. Our quarters were a corrugated metal hut called a Quonset or Nissen hut. It was the shape of a large barrel cut in half, long ways, half round. Probably twenty-five feet long, twelve feet wide and twelve feet high. It had a wooden wall on each end with a door in the front and cots enough for two – six men crews. We had a wood burning, pot-bellied stove in the middle of the room. There was one hanging light bulb and a concrete floor. Our mattresses were made of straw and covered with a canvas called "ticking." No sheets or pillowcases, just thick and itchy Army issue woolen blankets. Toilet facilities and bath had to be hiked to. We selected our beds, then after making them up, we fell in exhaustion for a good night's sleep.

There were two crews of us in our hut. We met the other crew in the morning. They were ending their tour and had perhaps four or five missions left. They had many a scary story to relate to us, including the first raid on Berlin by U.S. bombers, which was March 4, 1944. Because of weather, all groups were recalled; however, the 95th lead commander ignored, or pretended to not hear the recall and continued on with the mission.

The clouds over the target were so intense they broke up the formation. As their ship came out of a cloud, they found themselves directly behind a B-17 and they were caught in its prop wash. Immediately, they went into a flat spin at 19,000 feet.

While in the flat spin, the waist gunner said he was stuck to the roof, along with his parachute and a box of ammo. His mind kept saying, "Grab the chute and bail out." but he could not move because of centrifugal force. The pilot and copilot finally were able to push the controls forward at 5,000 feet and brought their ship out of the flat spin. They brought the ship home intact and with all their crew, although the rivets were pulled and the sheet metal wrinkled. The plane was scrapped.

The waist gunner lost it and became known as "Flakkie." If anyone would come up behind him and clap his hands, "Flakkie" would throw his hands up and scream. So, of course, they did!

Our new found home in England was beautifully green, but we seldom saw the sun through the clouds and rain. Eventually, we were scheduled to fly a training familiarization flight over England with a combat pilot. For that day's flight, we were assigned to an old F model B-17 called, "Patches." Believe me, it had plenty of patches, and it no longer flew combat missions. You might say it was war weary, tired and retired.

While we were standing on the hardstand, or parking ramp, for "Patches," our training pilot drove up in a jeep. As he was getting out of his jeep, we heard a loud roar and looked up to see the front half of a B-17 flipping downward out of the skies. It crashed and the tail section came after it out of the clouds, as well as one lone parachute. Nine men did not make it.

Minutes later, while we were discussing the incident, a second B-17, front half only, came flipping out of the clouds and crashed. The tail section followed it out of the clouds. Then, four parachutes; six more men did not make it. The two planes had a mid-air collision which happened all too often in those clouds. We were all so shaken up that our training pilot canceled our flight. **IT ONLY TAKES ONE.**

Eventually it was time to do what we were sent there to do – go to war. Wake up time was very early, depending on our mission. An orderly would enter our Nissen hut and individually awakened us with "Dancison's crew. You're flying." We would do our toilet, go to breakfast, and then to briefing for the target of the day.

For briefing, we would enter a smoke-filled room with fold up chairs and a large curtain hiding a huge map of Europe. When the briefing officer entered, we would be called to attention, then put at ease. The curtain would be drawn open to reveal England and the whole of Europe: France, Belgium, Holland, Denmark, Sweden, Germany, Russia, Italy, Spain, etc. Moans from everyone were standard procedure, for no target was considered a milk run because, **IT ONLY TAKES ONE.**

A string of yarn would designate our route and target for the day, along with secondary and third targets should target number one be overcast and unbombable. Heavy flak areas were pointed out, along with possible fighter encounters. After briefing, we would check out our parachutes, life jackets, and "Mae Wests." A jeep would take the gunners to armament, where we would pick up our guns. It would then take us to our ship where each gunner would install their guns. Our officers would arrive and we would board our ship. They would start engines, then taxi into a line of twenty or more ships (seven each from three squadrons). One squadron would stand down for repairs. We would line up on the runway and wait for a green flare. Then, at thirty-second intervals, we would start our roll.

Takeoff was generally under a low hung cloud cover, making the morning misty and gray with foreboding darkness. In a very short time, we would be airborne into the clouds and into a dark and lonely world of our own. It was like being in a graveyard at midnight. We could see nothing. The anticipation of something happening was ever present.

To regress a bit, flying conditions in England were very hazardous due to the many airfields of heavy bombers, medium bombers, and fighter planes both American and English. Airfields were located so close together, the only way planes could avoid hitting one another was to corkscrew directly over one's own field at a given rate of speed and climb. If an engine was lost, it was almost a sure crash. Clouds normally ranged from one football field high to three football fields high from the ground.

Once off the ground, we would fly blind into clouds ranging to an altitude of up to 16,000 feet before exiting them. This meant we flew blind for one to two hours. At last, we would burst through the clouds into a diamond clear display of sunshine and endless rolling white billowy clouds. The clouds would sparkle like a magic ocean in a fairy tale. Horizon to horizon, it stretched to infinity. We were entering the gates of heaven – and soon enough – HELL.

Prior to takeoff, I was given an Aldus signal lamp and was told to blink – DAH-DIT-DIT-DIT after takeoff, meaning "B" in Morse code. Once we exited the clouds, the blinking light identified our bomb group from other groups. Our pilot followed previous blinking Aldus lamps, which also displayed different colors of the day for the different positions or elements of our flight. We would then form together as a twenty-plane bomb group. After our get together in the sky, we would look for and rendezvous with two other groups, the 100th and 390th. The three formations formed a wing.

The 100th Bomb Group had the reputation of being the hardest hit group to fly in the ETO (European Theater of Operations). In fact, they were known as the "Bloody 100th."

They made a name for themselves, or so I was told, on the Regensburg-Schweinfurt raid on August 17, 1943. On that raid, 60 aircrafts were lost.

Whenever a plane was disabled and it did not appear the crew could make it back to England, the pilot would put his landing gear down to show the enemy he was surrendering.

On one occasion, A 100th pilot, or so it was said, put his wheels down. The navigator said it looked as though they could make it to the English Coast. There were two enemy aircraft that had flown in on each wing to escort the B-17 to one of the German airfields.

The pilot asked his waist gunners if they thought they could shoot both German planes down. The answer was affirmative. The pilot said, "Do it."

The German planes were shot down, but their pilots parachuted to safety. That night, Axis Sally went on the airwaves and said that she knew the group who had violated the rules of war. It was the big square D, the 100th Bomb Group. Axis Sally said the Germans would certainly retaliate.

The British and the Americans had an agreement. The Americans would bomb by day and the British would follow up by night. However, the British did not make the follow up that night to Regensburg-Schweinfurt on August 17, 1943. Instead, they bombed a coastal resort in Northern Germany. This location was Peenemunde on the Baltic Coast. It was where the Germans were experimenting with the V1 Buzz Bomb, the V2 rockets, the 262 Rocket Fighter Bomber plane, and Heavy Water (also known as the A Bomb).

Von Braun was the lead scientist at Peenemunde. He survived the bombing, but several other German scientists were killed.

After that, the Germans, in order to protect themselves, moved their scientific machinery into caves. With their rocketry, they were getting close to sending rockets into the United States so this bombing put a delay of several months into their program to attack the United States. England saved us, the United States of America, from experiencing war on our home front.

There were several very tough missions for the 100th that took place during and after the Regensburg-Schweinfurt raid. Of the sixty crews lost on the August 17, 1943 raid, nine were from the 100th and four were from the 95th.

Two months later, on October 8, 1943, the 100th lost seven crews over Bremen. Two days later, October 10, 1943, the 100th was sent to Munster. Twelve of thirteen crews sent out were lost. Only one crew returned to base.

An article from the *Alhambra Post-Advocate*

MISSIONS

MISSION 1 – DIJON, FRANCE

Our first mission that began our combat tour was Tuesday, April 25, 1944 to Dijon, France. We were awakened at 1:45 a.m. and went through what was to become our regular routine: toilet, breakfast and then briefing. After briefing, the gunners were taken to armament, picked up our guns and delivered them to our ship. Our guns had been cleaned by armament and were ready for installing.

Our crew positions had originally been assigned to us when we first met as a crew in Avon Park, Florida. I was given a waist gunner's position on that sheet, but spent all my time in the radio room and tail except for occasions of having climbed into the ball turret where I was never comfortable. I did not envy Leo, our ball turret gunner, who, in my opinion was the bravest man on the ship. Leo may scoff at me for what I say, but when I was down there, I felt like an egg, and every time our plane hit an air bump, I felt they cracked the egg and I was being dropped into the frying pan.

Luckily for me, the original tail gunner, Bob Rogers, never liked being alone and knew I loved the tail position. As we got off our delivery truck with our guns, Bob stepped up to me and said, "If you want the tail position, it's yours." At that moment I felt I was promoted, and even though it was to the rear of the ship, I could not have been happier. As I

38

crawled to the tail position and inserted my two guns, I looked down my gun sights and said to myself, "Come on you Nazi fly boys, I'm ready!!"

Unfortunately or fortunately, the German Luftwaffe found other guys to harass so we did not encounter any fighters, but if we had, I am sure I would have emptied both barrels in thirty seconds. Under the circumstances, our first mission could be termed, a "milk run," or easy mission.

Our ship, *Fireball* #231876. Time logged: eight hours and forty-five minutes. Our group position: Tail-Ass Charlie or Tail-End Charlie, meaning the last aircraft in formation. Opposition was light flak, no enemy fighters. We survived our first mission.

When we exited our plane, we were picked up by a 4 x 4 truck and taken to a debriefing room. There we were given a shot of Scotch and asked if we saw anything unusual. I commented I saw a B-17 at our altitude, with no markings and out of gun range.

This would become a common occurrence for most all our missions. The Germans captured our ships, then flew them at our altitude and related our air speed and altitude to their flak gunners below. We became sitting ducks with that kind of information.

MISSION 2 – BRUNSWICK, GERMANY

Wednesday, April 26, 1944, 12:45 a.m. Awakened for second mission. Target: Brunswick, Germany. We went through our routine: toilet, breakfast and then on to briefing. After briefing, the gunners trekked to armament where we picked up our guns. We then went to our "hard stand" where we had our first look at *Full House*, the ship we would end up flying in twenty-nine of our thirty-five missions. The ship was new to us, but had already been named by Crew Chief Alteri.

Time logged: seven hours and forty minutes. Position element lead. We had no fighter attacks but had considerable flak on the bomb run. Another milk run- but, **IT ONLY TAKES ONE.**

MISSION 3 – FLOTTEMANVILLE-HAGUE, CHERBOURG

Thursday, April 27, 1944, 1:35 a.m. Awakened for third mission. Target: Flottemanville-Hague, Cherbourg. This was a coastal bombing, I believe for submarines. We were the low element, Tail-Ass Charlie. The flak was precise and heavy.

Coastal flak was really the best the Germans offered. We were tracked by a series of four bursts, each fingering us as their target. I called the copilot and said, "Ruby, do something or they are going to get us."

We got a series of three-four bursts. The second four bursts crawled up on us, and the third series of bursts meant doomsday.

What happened next- I looked up and we were underneath the whole group with bomb bay doors open above us and we were already two minutes into the bomb run, the bombs ready to drop and me thinking double jeopardy.

Whatever fate is, our pilot, Dancison, cut our power as if we slammed on the brakes in the sky and flipped our plane out of the bomb run.

As he flipped the plane, the last series of four flak bursts, burst where we should have been with two loud "WHOOMHS." I heard the spray of flak on the bottom side of our plane. Our copilot, Ruby, said, "Wow!! That was meant for us!!" My thoughts were, "If you only knew!"

We dropped our bombs in the channel and returned home, tail between our legs.

Ship: *Full House*, Flying time: five hours and thirty minutes.

IT ONLY TAKES ONE. So far, so good.

MISSION 4 (SAME DAY) – LA CULOT, FRANCE

Thursday, April 27, 1944. Immediately after landing, we were informed we were to go on another mission. We were interrogated, ate, briefed and had just enough time to oil our guns and install them after takeoff.

How the pilot and copilot made it for lack of sleep and exhaustion, I do not know. Crew checkup was made at 17,000 feet. I was asleep and woke up when they called my name. I put on my oxygen mask, then checked out my guns.

On this particular mission, we had a supervisory pilot, Captain Gunn, to check out our pilot's flying ability for possibly making him the leader of the low squadron.

Targets A and B were heavily overcast so we went on to target "C," Target Le Culot, Belgium. We were credited with good bombing. Time flown: six hours and fifteen minutes. Ship: *Full House*. Total hours flying time for the day: eleven hours forty-five minutes.

MISSION 5 - SOTTEVAST, CHERBOURG, FRANCE

Friday, April 28, 1944. Went to bed at 12:00, midnight, and awakened at 3 a.m. Whole crew dead tired. Target: Sottevast, Cherbourg, France, military installations. Flak so intense over target, it broke up our formation resulting in a dry run. Almost went back but decided it was suicide so called it a day. Ship: *Full House*. Time logged: Five hours. Position purple heart corner. We were credited for a mission.

MISSION 6 – BERLIN

Saturday, April 29, 1944. Awakened at 2:45 a.m. Berlin was our target. The first Berlin bombing was March 4, 1944 by our 95th Bomb Group and 100th Bomb Group.

Today's Berlin mission was the seventh since March 4. We were exhausted but the receiving end had to be tougher.

On takeoff, our bomb load and armament was so heavy, the copilot had to hit all four super chargers to get us airborne. We were brushing treetops and I was pushing the floor of the plane to get it to rise.

We were not in our regular aircraft, *Full House*. We were in a more heavily armored ship called, *Knock Out Baby*, also known as "Armored Baby," because of the extra protective armament. It took two very skilled pilots just to get through the preliminaries. Luckily, we had two of the best!!

We encountered meager flak to the target; however, Berlin was not very receptive to us and formed a dark cloud of black smoke mingled with angry red flashes and noise enough to let us know there were two sides of the equation. Then, because of poor navigation, we hit more intense flak over Brunswick and Hanover which we were warned to miss.

Ship: *Knock Out Baby*. Time logged: Nine hours and fifteen minutes.

MISSION 7 - SARREGUEMINES, FRANCE

Monday, May 1, 1944. Late takeoff, 2:30 p.m. Sarreguemines, France. Target: marshalling yards (train depots). Encountered approximately seven ME 109s. Got off a short burst of a few hundred rounds. I was not nervous, just ready.

Ship: *Full House*. Landed: 9:30 p.m. Time logged: Seven hours.

MISSION 8 – SCRUBBED

Thursday, May 4, 1944. Target for today: Berlin. Scrubbed after takeoff because of weather.

PASS – LONDON

Friday, May 5, 1944. Received a two-day pass to London. Stayed at Brighton Hotel in Russell Square. Several of our crew stayed together for dinner at a local restaurant. I saw wild duck on the menu and ordered it. It must have been a German duck because on my first bite, I bit into a mouth full of feathers and at least twenty BBs. All of London must have been zeroed in on him. Yuck!!

MISSION 8 - BERLIN

Monday, May 8, 1944. Target: Berlin. Takeoff: 6:00 a.m. The flak was very intense. Seemed all flak guns turned on us as flak literally blanketed the skies. The Luftwaffe was up but fortunately for us, they targeted other groups.

Ship: *Full House*. Time logged: Eight hours and twenty minutes. Another lucky day.

MISSION 9 – LAON, FRANCE

Tuesday, May 9, 1944. Target: Laon, France. Takeoff 6:10 a.m. Airfield.

Ship: *Full House*. Time logged: Five hours and twenty minutes. Intense flak. No fighters.

MISSION 10 -- SCRUBBED

Wednesday, May 10, 1944. Target: Fallersleben Germany. Takeoff: 5:30 a.m. A cloudy day. Rendezvous 15,000 feet. Copilot Keeler asked if I could see our wingman. I replied, "He was just out of the clouds zeroing in on us." Then, out of nowhere, we encountered intense fog. Copilot, Ruby said, "Where'd this come from?" We were totally fogged in. All of a sudden, we encountered noise of other aircrafts and we were rocked with heavy prop wash. Our copilot, Ruby, said, "We just flew through a whole formation of other aircrafts- Like flak." To see flak is scary. To hear it puckers your butt. But to fly through a whole formation of other aircraft, hear their engines and experience their prop wash, missing one another was a miracle. I believe we had several.

Our pilot, Dancison found a hole in the clouds, an eye in the sky. We normally bombed between 23,000 feet and 26,000 feet, but we were now at 29,000 feet all alone. Danny said to us, "You should feel these controls, they are like mush!!"

The mission was scrubbed and somehow we found our way back to base. We circled down over our base and came out of the clouds about two football fields from the ground. How these young pilots and navigators brought us home is a miracle.

MISSION 10 - LIÈGE, BELGIUM

Thursday, May 11, 1944. Target: Liège, Belgium, marshalling yards. Takeoff: 2:55 p.m.

Ship: *Full House*. Landed: 8:25 p.m. Time logged: five hours and thirty minutes. Intense flak. Another lucky day.

MISSION 11 - BRUX, CZECHOSLOVAKIA

Friday, May 12, 1944. Target: Brux, Czechoslovakia. Oil field.

The mission, our longest to date, was to a large oil refinery. It was a clear, beautiful day. One could see for miles.

Having an early awakening at 1:30 a.m. and an early takeoff, I found myself half-asleep with the drone of engines when all of a sudden I saw the sky full of parachutes. The parachutes I saw were both German and American- yellow, black and white. They completely filled the skies behind me. There were so many that I could not even count them.

I checked in with the copilot, Ruby, and asked if there was a paratroop invasion going on. We were in the sandwich of three wings. Each wing had 60 ships. Ruby said, "You should see the lead wing. They are getting the crap shot out of them." Why he had not relayed us this information, I will never know.

From my tail position, I could press my face against my Plexiglas side window and I could see forward to about eleven o'clock on one side and one o'clock on the other. I could not see the twelve o'clock position.

What I could see looked like a beehive of battle engagements, not real but like a movie.

We had no fighter escort because wing tanks were not yet available to our fighters and we were too far from home base for our fighters to protect us.

Our B-17s were falling out of the sky as well as the German fighter planes. One German Focke-Wulf 190 fighter plane passed us fully engulfed in flames. I watched as he made a big diving arc. When he hit the ground, I thought he would never stop crashing. He just kept tumbling and tumbling and tumbling.

We made our bomb run on a perfectly clear day but for whatever reason, our lead bombardier failed to drop his bombs which meant we had to make a second bomb run.

On the second time around, we were zeroed in on. A round of flak nailed us but did not explode. It went through the bottom of our ship and severed a coil of wire 4 to 5 inches around. The flak also went through the pant leg of our top turret engineer and ripped open his parachute.

The shell did not explode on impact and we survived a direct hit.

Luckily, no one was severely hurt, but we no longer had interplane communication; however, we still had all four engines.

As we left the target area, because of the long kneeling position on my bicycle seat in the tail, my legs started to cramp. I repositioned myself so that I sat facing forward and stretched out my legs.

While doing this maneuver, I looked up at one of our aircrafts and saw

Not 3, Not 2, But 1 Engine Brings Crippled Fort Home

A FORTRESS STATION, May 17—The crew of the Pegasus, a B17 named after the fabled winged horse, told today how their damaged ship covered the last 200-mile lap home to Britain on one engine Friday after attacking the synthetic oil plant at Brux, Czechoslovakia.

Nearing the home stretch on its 32nd mission, the Pegasus had two engines knocked out by spitting cannon and machine-gun fire over France.

Blinded by the spray of oil on the windshield, 2/Lt. Clair E. Wyrick, of Alvordton, Ohio, jockeyed the Fort out of formation and headed alone for his base.

Then, flying at 12,000 feet, the No. 3 engine ran out of gas when the ship was 200 miles from home.

Working frantically while rapidly losing altitude, Wyrick tried to transfer gas from his useless left side to the right tank, but discovered that the Nazi fighters had drilled the fuel lines.

In an effort to lighten the ship, crewmen tossed almost everything portable overboard but retained several of the guns as a safeguard against sneak attacks.

Just when it looked as if the flying horse was about to give up, the English coast slipped by and Wyrick landed on an RAF field.

Other members of the crew are: Sgt. Willard C. Dale Jr., tail gunner, Sanborn, N.Y.; Sgt. Frankie Loscalzo, ball turret gunner, San Jose, Cal.; S/Sgt. Lee E. Garner, left waist gunner, Greenville, S.C.; Sgt. Carl J. Woodward, right waist gunner, Cullman, Ala.; S/Sgt. Abner C. Barfield Jr., radio operator-gunner, Kenly, N.C.; S/Sgt. Kenneth C. Bennett, top turret gunner, Harriman, N.Y.; 2/Lt. Hollie G. Flippen Jr., bombardier, Detroit, Mich., and 2/Lt. Alois T. Braje, navigator, Chicago.

Another Fort Lands Safely Thanks to Its 'Chute Brakes

A FORTRESS BASE, July 11—Crash trucks were sent onto the runway when a B17 piloted by 1/Lt. John M. Bastion, of Port Arthur, Tex., radioed it had to land without brakes. But not a single crewman was injured as the ship, joining The Stars and Stripes 'chute landing club, came to a stop with parachutes billowing from it.

---

4 Oil Plants Hit Deep in The Reich

1 in Czechoslovakia Also Pounded; Cost Is 42 Bombers, 10 Fighters

One of the strongest forces of American heavy bombers and fighters ever sent against German targets thundered across Europe yesterday to attack four major synthetic-oil plants in the Leipzig area of Germany and one at Brux, inside Czechoslovakia. In addition, the aircraft repair plant at Zwicklau, south of Leipzig, was hit.

Nearly 1,000 Fortresses and Liberators, escorted by as many Mustangs, Thunderbolts and Lightnings, were engaged in the operation.

Battling through savage resistance from enemy fighters, the planes bombed their targets with excellent results, photographs taken during the operations indicated. Forty-two American bombers and ten fighters failed to return.

While some formations encountered fierce opposition, others saw not a single enemy plane. The force which went to Brux said as many as 200 interceptors of all kinds swept in, sometimes 40 or 50 at a time. American fighter pilots claimed 66 enemy aircraft shot down; bomber crews' claims had not been tabulated at a late hour.

One fighter pilot, 1/Lt. Robert J. Rankin, of Washington, reported shooting down five—the second pilot in the ETO to make such a score.

Leipzig is an estimated 550 airline miles from London, and Brux 650.

Articles from *Stars and Stripes*, our European newspaper, after Brux, Czechoslovakia about our group, "the 95th Bomb Group" smoke and figured the plane was about to feather an engine. Then I observed the smoke was coming in puffs. I opened my side window and heard gunfire. I pressed my face to the Plexiglas and looked forward to see the prettiest circus of Focke-Wulf 190s slow rolling and firing twenty-millimeter cannons at us. I looked inside, past our tail wheel to the waist. There were our two waist gunners smoking cigarettes and punching one another on the shoulder like they were reminiscing about London and the Piccadilly Circus. They were totally unaware of the German attack.

I broke my cartridge belt apart and threw approximately five rounds of ammo at them but could not get the ammo past the tail wheel.

I quickly reattached my ammo belt and, as a Focke-Wulf 190 flew past, I fired a parting shot. He did not stick around to thumb his nose at me, but immediately did a ninety degree dive straight down. There was no way I could have hit him, but I did alert the crew to bandits in the area. These were Goering's elite yellow-nose Focke-Wulf fighters. They did not stick around for a second pass. We were lucky.

Over France, the sky was so clear that I left the tail and went to the waist. For some reason, I figured we were at 10,000 feet or lower. As I talked to one of the waist gunners, I said, "Are we passing through a cloud? It is getting dark." He said, "We are at 23,000 feet!" He took off his oxygen mask and pushed it to my face. I was experiencing anoxia from lack of oxygen.

Without further incident to us, we completed our mission in *Full House* in nine and a half hours; however, other aircrafts in our group were having miraculous experiences of their own.

Three other planes from our group made *Stars and Stripes,* our combat paper in Europe, with their heroic endeavors. Their engines were shot out and they made their return to England on not three, not two, but one engine. They landed at an emergency air base on the English Coast. Two B-17s went around as prescribed, but the third was out of gas and altitude, so it made a direct-in-landing. That put two planes landing in one direction and the third landing in a head on collision.

The tail gunner I was talking to said the pilot rang the bailout bell on the runway. He, the tail gunner, went out the tail door. He told me he rolled and rolled and rolled some more. Only his sheep lined clothes saved him from being hurt badly. When he finally stopped, he looked up and the planes came to a stop nose to nose.

On this mission, we lost forty aircrafts and four hundred men. **IT ONLY TAKES ONE**. Our crew slipped through the cracks – another lucky day!

MISSION 12 - BERLIN

Friday, May 19, 1944. Target: Berlin. 9:00 a.m. takeoff. Encountered ME 109s and FW 190s.

Flak as usual was heavy, but we managed to fly through it. Today's flak contained several red bursts.

If the fighters are not giving you trouble, then the flak has a way of puckering your behind. When you see the flak burst, you think, "That was not just a puff of smoke." There are hundreds of pieces of shrapnel you cannot see. Each piece engraved with the words, "To Whom It May Concern."

Ship: *Full House*. Landing time: 6:05 p.m. Time logged: Nine hours and thirty-five minutes. Tenth time Berlin bombed. Our third Berlin mission.

MISSION 13 – BRUSSELS, BELGUIM

Thursday, May 25, 1944. Target: Brussels, Belgium, marshalling yards. Takeoff was at 4:56 a.m. Really sweated this number. We did not encounter any fighters and very meager flak. It was a milk run.

Ship: *Full House*. Landed: 10:40 a.m. Time logged: five hours and forty-five minutes.

PASS - LONDON

Saturday, May 27, 1944. Pass- Piccadilly Circus, London. Stayed at the Regent Palace Hotel. Visited Buckingham Palace and Westminster Abbey with waist gunner Langford. Returned Monday, May 28.

MISSION 14 – BRUSSELS, BELGIUM

Tuesday, May 30, 1944. Target: Brussels, Belgium- Again, marshalling yards (train depots). Takeoff: 7:15 a.m. Tracking flak, no fighters. Ship: *Full House*. Landing time: 11:45 a.m. Another milk run.

Of course, remember, even a milk run requires takeoff with a normal bomb load of twelve-five hundred pound bombs and 2780 gallons of gas as well as the climb through clouds, rendezvous with the 100th and 390th to form our wing and then the flight over the Channel to our target. Then the bomb run itself, the return to base and the descent through the clouds to the runway. All the time worrying about enemy aircraft coming in on you while you are flared out for a landing and all crew members crowded into the radio room.

Dancison, our pilot, told me he wanted me in the tail on landings and takeoffs. Other bases had been attacked and he wanted to be prepared.

MISSION 15 – "NO BALL," FRANCE

Friday, June 2, 1944. Target: "No Ball," France. Takeoff: 9:00 a.m.
"No Ball" was termed as coastal bomb installations or V1 or V2 rocket launching sites. Again, coastal targets had Germany's best flak shooters, defending their area with rocket type missiles.
Ship: *Full House*. Landing 1:23 p.m.
Looks like we are softening coastal installations. Maybe we are getting ready for D-Day.

MISSION 16 - D-DAY

Tuesday, June 6, 1944. D-Day. Takeoff: 7:00 a.m.
Our 95th Bomb Group put up three groups to overfly the invasion. We were in the middle group. Another crew took our *Full House* ship on the first encounter, so we ended up with another ship, #1989. We had engine troubles so we switched to an old "F" model, *Taint a Bird II*.
The skies were so overcast; we saw nothing of the invasion except for a few breaks in the clouds where a few ships and their white wakes could be seen in the middle of the channel. We missed the entire D-Day invasion. The day was so overcast that we did not drop our bombs but returned with them to our base.
Our mission did count even though we did not drop our bombs. Germany did not put up a single plane. The skies belonged to us.
Landing time: 12:00 p.m. Time logged: five hours.

MISSION 17 – DAY AFTER D-DAY

Wednesday, June 7, 1944. The day after D-Day. Takeoff: 3:35 p.m. Target: Bridge- Nantes, France.
Today we had better weather and we saw the invasion fleet and the invasion coast from 21,000 feet; however, we were too high to see any of the ground battles.
Ship: *Full House*. Landed: 11:05 p.m. Time logged: seven hours and forty minutes.

MISSION 18 - SCRUBBED

Saturday, June 10, 1944. Target: An airfield in France.
Our rendezvous was to be at 21,000 feet but weather was so bad that we ended up at an altitude of 27,000 feet. Vapor trails and clouds finally caused us to scrub the mission.

MISSION 18 - FRANCE

Monday, June 12, 1944. Target was termed a tactical mission which was an airfield in France. Takeoff was 4:35 a.m., which meant an early breakfast. At 10,000 feet, Ruby, our copilot, called to the waist and asked for an ammo box or something because his stomach was doing flip-flops. I called in too and said, "Make it two." My stomach was also flipping. We squatted and filled them. The smell was horrific, so what to do with the boxes? We opened the waist window and threw out both boxes, knocking off Rogers' front gun sight. Rogers was pissed, but the recipients below must have come up with adjectives of their own. We proceeded on. I might add that undressing from our jumpsuits at minus sixty-degree weather is a very chilly experience.

Our original target was overcast so we toured France looking for a target of opportunity. The Ack Ack, or flak, gunners followed our every move, but somehow we out maneuvered them. We dropped our bombs on an airfield at Arras, France, a target of last resort.

Ship: *Full House*. Landed: 10:04 a.m. Time logged: six hours and another mission.

MISSION 19 – ST. TROND, BELGIUM

Wednesday, June 14, 1944. Target for today: An airfield at Saint Trond, Belgium. Takeoff: 3:55 a.m. As like so many previous days, it was heavily overcast, so we went on to bomb our secondary target, another airfield at Chièvres, France. After bombs away, we discovered half our bomb load was still hung up, so we left the formation and salvoed, or released, them in the Channel.

We landed a half hour late to find our ground crew sweating us out.

Ship: *Full House*. Landed: 9:55 a.m. Logged: six hours and forty-five minutes.

Lost one 412 ship, Wells, the pilot from our training group from Avon Park, Florida.

MISSION 20 – HANOVER, GERMANY

Sunday, June 18, 1944. Target: Hanover, Germany. Takeoff: 5:20 a.m.

Another day with the clouds in the target area, supposedly two-tenths. However, when we hit the IP (Initial Point which is the start of a bomb run), the clouds were so heavy over and under us that we lost track of the other squadrons and dropped our bombs early. The results are unknown.

Ship: *Full House*. Landed: 11:45 a.m. Logged six and a half hours. Heavy flak, no fighters.

On the way, our wingman, *The Key Bird*, caught fire and immediately pulled out of formation. Our navigator, Frank Morrison, asked me to count the chutes. I counted eight before they were too far behind and out of sight. We were over the Channel, and to my knowledge, there were no survivors.

PASS - LONDON

Monday, June 19, 1944. Two day pass to London. June 13th was the first V-1 bombing of London.

On this date, June 19, 1944, the V-1 bombs flew over us and had us ducking in and out of our air raid shelters with regularity. Now we know what it is like to be on the receiving end. Of course, the V-1 was not an accurate bomb. It had its own motor and made an irregular sound because it only had a single cylinder motor. When it ran out of fuel, the motor stopped and it turned down into a bomb. It was a "To Whom It May Concern" type of bomb.

The V-1 flew at an altitude of almost five hundred feet and at a slow rate of speed, probably 150 to 200 miles per hour. If a spitfire aircraft would spot a V1, it would catch up to it and flip it over with its wings.

Once, on a return from one of our missions, I spotted one as it flew into a vacant field and exploded.

Later, I believe it was August of 1944, the V-2 was put into action. It had a rocket motor and flew very high and fast, possibly five hundred miles per hour.

MISSION 21 – PARIS, FRANCE

Friday, June 23, 1944. Target: Paris, France. Takeoff: 3:00 p.m.

We flew over the invasion coast today again, past Cherbourg and over Caen. The coast was jammed with US war ships. Cherbourg was still putting up flak. All of France looked war torn and cratered from our incessant bombings. We were sent into bomb at 19,000 feet, where as our normal bombing altitude was 23,000 feet to 26,000 feet. At 19,000 feet, we were a turkey shoot. Over the target and ten minutes past, the flak was extremely intense and more accurate than I have seen or heard it, even more so than in Berlin. When you hear flak and bump from the turbulence, you wonder which one is going to nail you. We bumped through Paris. It was scary.

The lead ship of the group directly behind us (could have been the 100th or 390th) got a direct hit by the flak and made a straight down nosedive. There was no way for anyone to survive.

We had several flak holes, and lost two spark plugs due to flak. Again, our guardian angel rode our mission with us.

The receipt for my hotel stay in London, May 27-29, 1944

Part of the buzz-bomb that struck the empty annexe Regent Palace Hotel, London, being removed by Home Guards.

Taken two weeks after our pass to London

Our bombing results were excellent. An oil storage depot in Paris could still be seen billowing up black smoke from the coast.

Ship: *Full House*. Landed: 8:45 p.m. Encountered no enemy aircraft.

MISSION 22 - LEIPZIG, BÖHLEN

Thursday, June 29, 1944. Target: Leipzig, Böhlen. Takeoff: 4:00 a.m.

The sky was the clearest ever over the target, yet we made three bomb runs before dropping our bombs. Not once in twenty minutes did we get out of range of their flak gunners. You pucker and pucker and pucker.

The first run, the bombardier said he did not have time to synchronize.

On the second run, he brought us over another bomb group so we had to make a third run. Thankfully, we had excellent bombing results. Thirteen of twenty aircrafts sustained battle damage. Only one B-17 was lost.

Again, *Full House* lucked out, but we were beginning to wonder about our odds.

Landed: 12:00 p.m. Time logged: Eight hours of fly time. Encountered approximately seven ME 109s which made one pass but left in a hurry when our escorts showed up.

PASS - LONDON

Monday, July 3, 1944. Another two day pass to London, and once again, buzz bombs continued to rain on us making London very uncomfortable.

MISSION 23 - KÖLLEDA, GERMANY

Friday, July 7, 1944. Target: Kölleda, Germany. Takeoff: 5:10 a.m.

Full House was in the hanger for repairs, so we flew another aircraft, *Ready Freddy*.

We made a dry run over our primary target, a synthetic oil plant at Merseburg, Germany, because of intensive tracking flak. We also made a dry run over our secondary target which was an airfield.

Our bombing of Kölleda, Germany was termed excellent.

Landed: 12:00 p.m. Logged: six hours and fifty minutes.

MISSION 24 - MUNICH, GERMANY

Tuesday, July 11, 1944. Target: Munich, Germany, buzz bomb factories.

July 10th, my birthday, we were not posted to fly.

My navigator, Frank Morrison, brought me a fifth of Scotch to celebrate. I passed it around our Nissen hut and everyone took a swig. I finished off the bottle and happily went to bed. They posted our crew to fly after 10:00 p.m.

Takeoff was 8:30 a.m. They say oxygen is a good way to shake off a hangover- I do not remember.

While over the target, I watched a direct hit on one of our aircrafts piloted by First Lieutenant Jack Bertrum. I thought for sure they were goners.

The plane lost one engine. My very good friend from gunnery school, "Snake" Carpenter, from Stockton, California, was the waist gunner. He was hit on the shoulder by a burst of flak. Luckily for him, he had just picked up a flak vest and threw it over his shoulder. A piece of shrapnel did penetrate the vest and wounded him enough so that it ended his combat tour and he was sent home.

They made it home on three engines, late and alone.

Ship: *Full House*. Landed at 4:35 p.m. Time logged: nine hours and five minutes flying time.

24 MISSIONS COMPLETED

With twenty-four missions in, our missions were upped from twenty-five to thirty missions by General Jimmy Doolittle.

MISSION 25 - MUNICH, GERMANY

Wednesday, July 12, 1944. Target: Munich, Germany. Takeoff: 8:30 a.m. Target: A Focke-Wulf assembly plant. Encountered heavy flak over the target.

Our radio had four settings. The first was interplane, the second was intergroup, the third was command, and the fourth was liaison. On the return home, our copilot told us to turn our aircrafts' voice setting to command.

Command let us hear what the Germans were saying about our bombing raids. Their radio announcer said we were dropping a lot of duds. Unknown to them, these were timed bombs to go off at a later hour. Such is war.

Ship: *Full House*. Time logged: Nine hours combat time.

MISSION 26 - STUTTGART, GERMANY

Sunday, July 16, 1944. Target: Stuttgart, Germany. Takeoff: 5:30 a.m.

Primary target was Munich, Germany, but the target was overcast so we went on to the secondary target, Stuttgart, Germany. Bombing results were unknown.

Ship: *Full House*. Landed: 1:05 p.m. Logged: eight hours fly time.

FUN TIME

Monday, July 17, 1944.

Copilot Ruby checked out an L-4B (Piper Cub) and asked if I would care to see the base close up from the air. Naturally, I said, "Yes."

Ruby is a very careful pilot, but we still did some fun maneuvers and then came in for a landing. Ruby was used to kicking the rudder of a B-17, so, on landing, he kicked the rudder. We landed sideways. He said, "Oh shit!!" and kicked the rudder again giving us a hundred and eighty degree sideways landing. Luckily, we did not crash, but we did create a little excitement between us. We had a good laugh after.

Between the two, I think I would prefer to stick to combat flying; fun flying can get you killed!

MISSION 27 - HEMMINGSTEDT, GERMANY

Tuesday, July 18, 1944. Target: Hemmingstedt, Germany, oil storage tanks. Takeoff: 4:45 a.m.

Target completely overcast, so we bombed by Pathfinder Force (PFF), a new method of bombing through clouds by radar. Results: Unknown.

Ship: *Full House*. Logged: six and a half hours.

"READY FREDDY"

Wednesday, July 19, 1944.

I had a very good friend whom I met in gunnery school that had taken a liking to me. He invited me to get out early one morning. We took a walk in the back sections of farmland. We went into a chicken coop and picked up four eggs, two each. We took them back to our base kitchen and cooked them. Fresh eggs are a real treat when only powdered were available.

On this date, July 19, 1944, my friend, a radio operator, came to our Nissen hut and was crying. I asked what happened and he told me he had lost his entire crew.

His pilot, Sasser, had fighter pilot friends who had come to visit him and they wanted to ride in a heavy bomber. They wanted my friend's space, so they asked if he would mind relinquishing it to one of the fighter pilots.

They buzzed their P-47 base with full self-sealing (Tokyo) tanks and hooked a wing on a beacon light. They crashed and exploded, killing all on board.

Like the Piper Cub episode, fun flying is where the dangers are -- and you do not get combat mission credit.

MISSION 28 - LUTZKENDORF, GERMANY

Thursday, July 20, 1944. Target: Lutzkendorf, Germany, (Leipzig) oil storage tanks. Target again overcast. Bombed by PFF (Path Finder). Takeoff: 6:30 a.m.

Ship: *Full House*. Landed: 2:00 p.m. Logged: eight and a half hours. Heavy flak. No fighters.

One waist gunner, Rogers, taken off crew, leaving us with a nine-man crew.

MISSION 29 – CADILLAC, FRANCE

Tuesday, August 1, 1944. Target: Cadillac, France, air drops to the French Maquis. Takeoff: 10:20 a.m. We flew into the Swiss Alps in southern France at (I believe) an altitude of 500 at the top of the mountain. We flew in formation with our landing gear and flaps down to lower our air speed. We dropped 3780 containers of who knows what to the free French. I recall multicolored chutes and little people scrambling for packages. Our ball turret gunner, Leo Makelky, said he remembered a huge wooden cross at the end of the valley and, in a frightened state, he was pushing up trying to give the plane a boost to clear the cross.

As we left the drop area, my heated suit burnt out and I froze on the return trip. This was the third time my suit burnt out and, at minus sixty degrees, you need all the heat you can muster.

The "F" model B-17 had open waist windows and the air funneled into the tail. I was lucky because they enclosed the windows in the "G" model, the ship we flew.

Ship: *Full House*. Landing: 7:20 p.m. Logged: nine hours and twenty minutes. No flak, no fighters.

Wednesday, August 2, 1944- Happy days. Missions upped from thirty to thirty-five.

MISSION 30 - FRANCE

Thursday, August 3, 1944. Takeoff was 12:10 p.m. With clouds at a supposed altitude of 2000 feet over the target, we went into France to bomb a bridge, but the clouds were not permitting. They ranged at an altitude of over 20,000 feet!

Caught some flak over Caen and came home without dropping our bombs.

The mission counted because we were in enemy territory and encountered flak.

Ship: *Full House*. Landed: 5:40 p.m. Logged: five hours and thirty minutes.

MISSION 31 – POLTAVA, RUSSIA

Sunday, August 6, 1944. Took off this morning on a shuttle mission to Russia called, "Frantic." Bombed an airdrome at Rahmel (Gdynia) in the Polish Corridor. Strangely, seven American P-47s flew over us clearly marked with German swastikas. They were near enough to be fired on but neither side fired. I never did hear if they were good guys or bad.

Over the target, we encountered German fighters and also saw red and green flak.

FW 190s made a frontal attack shooting 20mm cannon fire at us and only our top turret gunner fired back.

We had P-51 escorts with us, so after the Germans flew through us, the P-51s took over and scared the Germans away.

This was the second 8th Air Force shuttle run to Poltava, Russia, then to Italy and back home.

The first shuttle run to Poltava, Russia was in June of 1944. The B-17s were followed in by a German HE 177. That night, June 21, 1944, German bombers returned and bombed unopposed for about two hours without the loss of a single German aircraft.

They succeeded in destroying forty-three B-17s, damaging twenty-six B-17s and fourteen P-51s.

The in-charge Russians would not allow us to defend ourselves because the American propaganda would say the Russians could not defend themselves, and it would make them look bad.

As we circled the field for landing, we caught sight of the shot up American B-17s strewn all over the Poltava airfield. To my knowledge, we had not been apprised of the first shuttle catastrophe. It scared the be-Jesus out of me.

The airfield had PSP (porous steel planking) for a runway. PSP is an open grid of metal that formed a steel tarmac. It was used so we could take off and land on soft or muddy ground. But it had no traction, so it was like driving on ice. Our pilots landed on it, then carefully taxied to our parking area.

While getting out of my rear exit door, carrying my B2 bag in my right hand, a young Russian soldier came up to me, saluted and handed me a wrapped package. He must have thought I was the pilot. Wrong end of the airplane.

Since I was carrying my B2 bag in my right hand, I saluted with my left! (We often did that with our own pilots and thought nothing of it.) I looked over at my pilot, Dancison, and he rolled his eyes in disgust.

I quickly diverted attention to my pilot, which got me off the hook.

In the meanwhile, I was searching the skies for German aircraft and did a little puckering.

Our bombing at Rahmel (Gdynia), Poland was deemed good. We logged nine hours and forty-five minutes. Ship: *Full House.*

LEO'S STORY

After landing in Russia, Leo took off to the main gate. His father was Russian and escaped back in 1910.

The guard told Leo, "Stoy!" (meaning "Stop!"), and poked a bayonet in his back. An interpreter was brought up and advised Leo he was not at liberty to do any visiting. We thought they were our allies.

Young Russian boys about fourteen years of age delivered and loaded our bombs. They would drive up to the plane in a pick-up truck, turn the truck around, and accelerate so the bombs rolled out onto the ground. Then they would lift the bombs up physically and place them into the bomb racks.

I thought to myself that I did not want to stand around in case the bombs went off, so I got out of there fast!

Dinner that night was served by very stocky Russian farm girls. There were patches of snow on the ground and these girls were barefoot. Their sleeves were rolled up and they served us with big spoons from huge pots they carried under their arms. We received healthy servings from very healthy, bosomy girls.

That night, after dinner, a marvelous group of Russian musicians put on an outdoor concert which was something to remember. We got to see a lot of Russian dancing where they squatted and kicked out their legs. I believe it is called "The Cossack" dance.

After a nine hour and forty-five minute mission, we were happy to bed down. Patches of snow covered the ground. We slept on cots with only one blanket to protect us from the ice and frost. I froze.

MISSION 32 - TRZEBINIA, POLAND BACK TO POLTAVA

Monday, August 7, 1944. Took off from Poltava, Russia at 0600. The trip to the target was uneventful, except for moderate flak over the target. The target was an oil refinery at Trzebinia, Poland.

After bombs away, I watched the smoke rise to our altitude of 23,000 feet. Our bombs must have been right on. I also saw red flak and a few German fighters, but they did not attack us.

As we returned from Germany into Russian territory, our copilot, Ruby, announced, "We're at 10,000 feet. I'm off oxygen."

I slipped back from my tail guns and took off my helmet and oxygen mask. I massaged my ears, put on my head set and heard the pilot say to the copilot, "Grab it Ruby!! Grab it!!"

I looked back over the tail and saw we had pulled away from the group, and we were in a dive. I also saw two chutes go past my tail and got the feeling of, "Oh shit, we are abandoning the aircraft."

I looked forward past the tail wheel into the waist, but only saw heavy smoke. I immediately put on my chute and scooted past the tail into the waist.

Leo Makelky, the ball turret gunner had opened the waist window to clear the smoke. The aircraft seemed to be stable. I asked Leo, "Who bailed out?" Leo had not seen what I had seen, so he said, "Nobody."

In the meantime, the waist gunner, Langford, seeing all the smoke, grabbed a fire extinguisher and went through the bomb bay to the front of the ship with no parachute. Both the top turret gunner and Langford put out the fire with portable extinguishers.

We had had an oxygen blowout fire at the base of the top turret located at the transfer valves. The cause of the blowout was the constant rubbing of our oxygen hoses and the top turret being rotated in azimuth, eventually wearing out the hoses.

When the explosion and fire occurred, it sent a sheet of flames between the pilot and copilot into the nose of the ship where our navigator and bombardier were located. After thirty-two missions of combat flying, our sturdy leader panicked and left his seat. I will not judge him for this maneuver because panic is a moment's notice; no one knows when it could happen.

Fortunately, two crewmembers and the copilot brought the ship under control. They put out the fire and saved us all from bailing out. Those of us in the rear of the ship knew nothing of what was happening up front.

Our copilot, Ruby Keeler, returned the ship into formation and nothing more was said. Upon landing, nothing more was discussed, but it was evident that the pilot and copilot were at odds.

The next morning, our pilot, Dancison, asked me to check out one of the previous shuttle run planes, one that had been bombed and abandoned because of the German bombing in June.

A jeep arrived and took me to an aircraft. I inspected the plane starting from the tail, moving to the waist, then the radio room through to the pilot's compartment.

There had to be three to four inches of dirt on the floor and no maintenance had been done since the June of '44 bombing. It was a mess.

As I stepped out of the waist door, a jeep drove up with officers from another crew. Their pilot asked me if we were claiming the plane. I answered, "If you want it, it's yours. I think our plane, *Full House,* can be made to fly."

I returned to our pilot and said, "Another crew wanted the plane, and frankly there was no maintenance on it and I did not feel it airworthy."

Danny, our pilot, thanked me and somehow our plane was made to fly through spare parts from the June shuttle. The nose door was replaced, but the oxygen system did not get fixed, so we used "walk-around" oxygen bottles for our flight to Italy.

MISSION 33 – POLTAVA TO ITALY

Tuesday, August 8, 1944. Poltava, Russia to Italy.

Since we no longer had a navigator or bombardier, due to the fire and bailout, our pilot, Dancison, predetermined Leo to be a combination of both. Leo was a natural. As a navigator, he told the officers where to go when they peed on his ball turret window, icing it up so he could not see through it. Leo was also the armament gunner on our ship. He checked the bomb bay after our bomb release to see that there were no hang-ups.

The lead bombardier for the groups did the actual aiming. When the lead bombardier released his bombs, all Leo had to do was toggle our bombs on his release. Instant officer material.

With Leo up front and no longer in the ball turret, the pilot requested I fly the turret. No tail gunner. I flew only half the mission from Poltava to Italy in the ball. I was getting cold feet, literally, so I decided if I was going to freeze, I would do it in the comfort and security of my tail position. I would return to the ball only if requested to by my pilot.

Our target on this mission from Poltava to Italy was Buzău, Romania. We never saw the ground because of solid under cast. We bombed through clouds by PFF.

We were told our bombing was good.

We landed in Foggia One at the bottom of the boot of Italy after eight and a half hours of flying. What we saw was total devastation. There were no standing buildings anywhere, only rubble. Such is war.

Our first night in Italy we were assigned tents and cots to sleep in. My waist gunner, Langford, asked me to accompany him to the enlisted quarters of the British North African Army. There, we exchanged chevrons, 8th Air Force patches and any exchangeable items with a few rounds of Italian wine. Those British soldiers were truly great hosts, and we left them feeling no pain.

It was late when we returned to our tent and only Langford's cot was empty.

Danny, our pilot, was in my cot, so I decided I would sleep in our plane. The night was dark but I figured I could find our plane, so I took off across the airfield. All of a sudden, a flashlight caught me in its beam and the words "Halt! Who's there??" I explained my situation, we had just flown in from Poltava and I was going to sleep in my plane.

The guard said, "You dumb son of a bitch. I am supposed to shoot first, then ask questions!" He came up to me and said, "Stick with me. Maybe I can get us there without either of us getting killed."

With that, he began shouting at the other guards and waving his flashlight, saying, "Don't shoot. I've got one of those dumb 8th Air Force guys that just flew in and doesn't know the rules."

Well, I am still here. I slept in the waist of our plane and did not get shot. Again, my guardian angel was looking out for me.

Italy was pretty much bombed out and there was not much to offer. We spent four days there because of the weather. They offered us a truck and driver. He took several of us to the beach on the Adriatic. It was hard to imagine how a California teenager could be enjoying the benefits of the Adriatic Sea shores while there was a war going on.

8th Bombers Land At 15th Airdromes

MAAF HEADQUARTERS, Aug. 8—Heavy bombers of the 8th AAF which yesterday bombed a German factory in Poland on their way to Russia, today landed at 15th AAF bases after pounding two enemy airdromes in the Ploesti area of Rumania on the second leg of their triangle-shuttle flight.

All aircraft landed in Russia without loss yesterday after attacking a Nazi factory at Rahmel, 10 miles northwest of the Polish port of Gdynia. Few enemy aircraft were encountered, but flak was reported heavy at some points.

Airdromes in Rumania at Buzau and Zilistea were bombed today without serious interception, and British based escorting Mustangs reported one victory over the Luftwaffe. The attacks were the 20th such operation since shuttle bombing technique was inaugurated by 15th AAF on June 2.

An announcement today disclosed that 29 enemy aircraft were destroyed by fighters and bomber gunners participating in yesterday's 15th AAF raid on two synthetic oil plants at Blechhammer, in Silesia. In all operations, including medium and fighter bomber attacks in southern France, Italy and Yugoslavia, 22 Allied planes are missing.

Article from *Stars and Stripes*, about our group, "the 95th Bomb Group

MISSION 34 – ITALY TO ENGLAND

Saturday, August 12, 1944. Target: Toulouse, France airfield. Again, our pilot took off on PSP (porous steel planking). It does not give the traction of cement, so our copilot, Ruby, got us off with a shot of turbo super charger and a couple of puckers.

We had a good bomb run and trip. We settled back in to our routine and landed in England completing our shuttle.

The bomb mission was nine hours and fifteen minutes. It was good to be back home.

To add a little humor to our flight, someone had decided to store liquor from Italy in the radio operator's compartment because liquor was hard to get in England.

As we got to altitude, the bottle caps started to pop. Comeau, the radio operator, called Leo and said to come up, he had a problem.

So the two of them got together and did not invite any of the rest of us. So as not to waste any of the liquor, anything that spilled over, they drank.

Needless to say, when we landed, they were pretty well snockered.

It was a good thing that that part of our run was a milk run, or should I say a champagne run.

ENGLAND - 34 MISSIONS COMPLETED

With thirty-four missions in and minus our navigator and bombardier, base operations decided to give us a "rest leave" to await our two crewmen.

On Monday, August 14, 1944, our crew was sent to Southport, England, by Liverpool, for some R & R (Rest and Relaxation). R & R meant movies, poolside, food and sightseeing. It also included a bar if we wanted to drink.

When we first arrived, I recall that evening at the bar with our crew. We met two fighter pilots who flew P-38s.

I am not sure how the conversation developed, but we told them how, on one mission, we had engine trouble and left the formation over Germany on three engines.

We were all alone when this twin engine P-38 pulled up alongside of us with only one engine working. We escorted each other back to the channel, then broke off to our individual bases with a wiggle of our wings.

It turned out that we had both experienced the same situation, so it was only natural the question came up, "Do you remember the tail marking on the B-17??"

The P-38 pilot said, "I certainly do. The tail marking was a big square 'B'."

I do not know if somehow we tipped our tail marking off to him, but I like to believe it was chance. Besides, with a drink (or several), I would like to believe the world is flat, round, square, or whatever fits. Those fighter pilots toasted us and we toasted them. At the flak house, life was all camaraderie. If the Germans were there, we would have toasted them too.

When we returned to Horham, England, Morrison and Sherwood also returned from their circuitous trip from Poltava. My first question to Morrison was, "What happened when you met up with the Russians?"

Morrison related, while on decent in his chute, he saw a Russian outpost in the middle of nowhere. A line of trucks left the outpost and the first truck pulled up to him as he got out of his harness. Morrison's first reaction was to go to his escape kit under his jacket, where words could be translated from English to Russian.. For example, "I am an American. That's a B-17. I am your ally."

As he reached for his escape kit, he realized his motions could be interpreted as reaching for a 45 pistol hidden under his jacket.

With that thought, he threw up his hands and said, "Americonski, Americonski!!"

The Russian laughed and said in perfect English, "I'm a graduate of University of Michigan. I know those are B-17s. I returned home and was conscripted into the Russian Army."

Breakfast for Morrison and Sherwood was before 6:00 a.m. They bailed out at about 2:30 p.m. The Russians decided they would prepare a banquet for their guests, but it did not take place until 7:00 p.m. At the banquet, one of the Russians stood up and said, "A toast to the Americans!"

Each plate had a rather large glass filled with Vodka, so Morrison and Sherwood responded and drank as the Russians.

Then the second Russian stood up and said, "A toast to the Americans," and then the third until Morrison could no longer recall the situation, but a good time was had by all.

The following day, arrangements were made to return to Poltava and then back to England. It took two weeks, but they were returned to England safe and sound.

Meanwhile, our beloved, *Full House* was flown by a brand new crew. On their first mission to Zeitz, Germany, they were shot down by a 105 Flak gun and took another B-17 down with them. Such is the luck of the draw. First mission, middle mission, last mission- **IT ONLY TAKES ONE**.

For us, we only had one more mission to complete.

The logo on the B-17 our crew flew on for our final mission

MISSION 35 – BIG CHIEF ILLINIWEK

Friday, August 25th, 1944. Target: Politz, Austria.

Because of losing *Full House*, our crew chief, Master Sergeant Ferrari, obtained a brand new B-17 G. He named it *Big Chief Illiniwek* after the Indian warrior of Illinois history.

This was to be our ship for our final mission; its first. After briefing, we followed our regular routine. We picked up our guns and installed them, then waited for our officers to join us.

On their arrival, we all inspected our ship and were impressed by the newness of it all. We climbed aboard. Engines were started and we joined the long row of B-17s in line for takeoff. The usual cloud cover was hanging just over our heads, but this morning seemed like a dream.

Operations finally shot the green flare indicating our mission was a go. The lead ship took off and at thirty-second intervals, the rest of us followed. Each disappeared into the cloud cover above us.

Takeoff was always critical because of our heavy gas and bomb loads. Normal bomb loads are twelve-500 pound bombs or incendiaries and 2875 gallons of gas. It took two very good pilots to get us airborne. We had the best!!

After exiting the clouds at 15,000 feet, we formed our group, then our wing and headed out over the channel flying to our prescribed altitude towards our target.

However, over Germany, when we began to climb above 20,000 feet, number three engine of our new ship could not hold manifold pressure and we could not keep up with the group.

For the first time on our tour, we had to abort. We turned and headed home alone. Luckily, we encountered no enemy opposition.

As we got over the channel, our pilot dropped down to sea level where I spotted some enemy "seagulls."

I am not sure, but I would like to claim five probables, as I did a lot of shooting.

Leo did too. He burnt out both barrels and the crew chief, Master Sargent Farrari, was very impressed with the defense of his new ship.

We were given credit for our mission because we had entered German Territory. However, two 412th ships were lost to flak over the target, Hamawa and 898. One of them could have been us.

35 MISSIONS COMPLETE: COMBAT TOUR OF DUTY OVER

Like the crew of the *Memphis Belle* of the 8th Air Force, we slipped through the cracks.

In 1944, when we flew combat, chances of survival were one in five or twenty out of a hundred. Any time after the fifteenth mission, life was a flip of a coin.

Our guardian angel rode with us all the way.

While awaiting orders to ship home, I had procrastinated and then decided to take a chance on getting my clothes washed, as they were all dirty except for what I was wearing.

We had a thirteen-year-old laundry boy from the nearby town of Aye who collected our laundry. His mother washed and folded our clothes. We in turn, traded our laundry soap and a few shillings for her trouble.

I decided to turn over all my clothes to him at about 2:00 p.m., figuring I was good for one more day.

At 10:00 p.m. that night, my shipping out orders were posted for me to leave at 3:00 a.m. I had no clothes except for what I was wearing.

I had no choice. I had never been out to our nearby town of Aye and I did not know the name of our laundry boy or his family. But I had no choice; I had to find him.

I went to our navigator, Morrison, and asked to borrow a bicycle.

I peddled to the gate and asked for directions to town. I decided a pub was my only bet and, as luck would have it, I found one.

I entered and went directly to the bartender and told him my dilemma. Everyone in the pub stopped what they were doing. The Englishmen were throwing darts and drinking mild and bitters (beer), their wives and children sitting watching. Everyone immediately sensed my problem and all joined in to help me.

One woman said she thought the boy's name was Peter Brane and his mother was the laundry woman. All roads were dirt or paths, but they gave me directions. "It's only a short ride, Yank. Take the path outside and when you come to a haystack, turn right to a barn. Go left to a fence then right to a house."

Of course, that night was one of those completely dark nights. I've heard it said (in a psychology class at Mount. San Antonio City College years later) that most people's memory bank can hold up to seven things to remember, some more, some less. This is how phone numbers were established. My memory bank is <u>one</u> on a good day. Do not give me two items to remember, or I will forget them both!

I found the turns and the house and knocked on the door at midnight.

A young teenage girl opened a second story window shutter over my head and asked, "Who is it?"

I answered, "Larry Stevens from the 95th Bomb Group, and I was hoping I had the right family." Peter's head popped out and he said hello to me. He asked, "Why are you here?" I explained I was leaving for home at 3:00 a.m. and needed my clothes.

He said to me with a little intake of breath, "You mean- ugh- you're going home to the United States of- ugh- America?" He put a chill up my spine with his intake of breath!!

His mother appeared at the door and invited me in. She gathered my folded clothes and wished me the best. I will never forget those wonderful people, including those from the pub.

I made my 3:00 a.m. ship out on time and was put into a four by four truck and driven to the train station. Several of us were assigned a Pullman car and started our departure. Our train moved slowly and then we were shuttled to a sidetrack, as we were not priority. While waiting for other trains to pass by, I noticed some dim lights and an open-roof shed where we were waiting. I stepped down from the train and walked over to the shed and asked what they were selling. They said, "Chips (fried potatoes). Would you like to buy some?" I said, "Sure." I still had English money, but I was not sure of its worth. One pound was four dollars and ten shillings was two dollars, so I said, "Give me ten shillings worth."

They laid out several open newspapers and gave me a mound of chips. I carried the chips like I would hold a baby and stepped back into the train. I went to my seat and set them down. Everyone was staring at me. I said, "I can't eat all these by myself. Why don't we share them? Everyone, please help yourselves."

And they did! No one made a pig of himself and the entire car immediately became friends. Wow!! What a wonderful $2.00 investment!!

Eventually we arrived at the main army base in England, Stone Village. Leo Makelky was there and had gotten himself a runner's job in the orderly room which, when he left, he turned over to me.

In the meantime, to retrogress, I had one year of high school art and showed a small amount of talent. I was not creative, but I could copy.

Our pilot, Dancison, was the only married man on our ten-man crew. The ship we flew in was already named *Full House*, by the crew chief. Danny, our pilot, made up his own logo, "Naughty Nan," for his wife. I painted it on the back of his and my A2 leather jackets. The crew had me do the same on their jackets, all except the copilot. He preferred to paint his own jacket without the logo as he had his own girl. I included a small painting of a B-17 on the front of the jacket and eventually thirty-five bombs for our missions.

Back to Stone Village, I ran across a high school art class member from

Alhambra High School. He said he was sure glad to see me. He was stationed in Stone and had the corner on painting the A2 jackets. He said he could use my help. For every jacket I painted, I got $25.00. I believe I did three, and at that time, $25.00 was big money.

When Leo left, I took over his spot and stopped painting. I delivered messages all over the base.

One day at lunch, I got into the chow line and a young gunner came in right behind me. He was wearing buck sergeant stripes, three chevrons, where as I was wearing staff sergeant stripes, three chevrons and a rocker. Three chevrons meant you were brand new, a new arrival.

I asked him, "Are you coming or going?" He said, "I'm going. I only got in one mission and lost my entire crew. We were hit by flak over the target and had to come home alone with engine problems."

Over the channel, his pilot rang the bailout alarm. One person was standing at the rear door, so he pushed him out and went out after him. He said the plane exploded and knocked him out. He came to just above the channel waters. Looking around, he saw a touring car with three people. They stopped and grabbed a dory (a small boat) and paddled out to him. With their help, he climbed aboard and then went to help the person he shoved out, but the man had drowned at the end of his chute.

These were French people, two men and a woman. They got back into their car and started to point and say, "Americans, Americans!!" They could not speak English and the young gunner could not speak French. It was after D-Day so the Americans were already occupying France.

Eventually, the four of them stopped at a roadside inn and ate dinner. When they finished, all four went to rent rooms for the night. The two French men left for a separate room, leaving the young gunner and the woman in a room to themselves. The French woman walked over to the young gunners bed and stripped off all her clothes. She then climbed into bed.

"Wow!!" I said, "That's a chance of a lifetime. What did you do?"

He said, "I climbed into bed with all my flying clothes and did not move all night. In the morning, the two French fellows entered my room and asked what took place. They pointed at me and laughed. That was my life I was fooling with and I wasn't about to fool."

Me in jacket I painted for myself and 9 of my crewmembers

My copilot's A2 jacket which he hand painted

A close up of my copilot's jacket

Eventually my name was called and I had to leave. I flew in a C54, a four-engine transport plane and stopped in Iceland, Newfoundland and New York. In New York, my luggage was cursory searched and I was given an okay to "go on home and enjoy myself."

I believe I could have brought a German Fighter plane home and my inspector would have overlooked it. He was in awe and proud of me as a returned combat person. 'Course, I was wearing all my combat ribbons. He knew I had flown combat and survived. He truly wanted me to return home and enjoy America. To him, I was a hero.

The war was still on, so I signed up for a tail gunner's position on a B-25 to be sent to the Pacific. I was at a holding base waiting for assignment in Lincoln, Nebraska, on May 8, 1945, when the Germans surrendered. I was drinking milk in the PX (Post Exchange, on base) with eight combat returnees from England. They were all drinking beer. When the word went out that the Germans had surrendered, one fellow said, "I'm buying a round for the table." I declined and all the fellows said, "This is special. No way can you decline," so I said, "Okay. One beer!!"

Of course, you know how that goes. The said "Oh sure, you'll have one with him, but I'm not good enough." Eight beers later, I was standing in the latrine soaking my head in the washbasin.

I woke up in the morning with my bed on top of a two story barrack. I do not know how they got me up there, or how I got down. Only drunks could figure out how to do that.

ONE LAST TIME – GREENVILLE, NORTH CAROLINA

Eventually I got on a B2-5 crew with four officers, pilot, copilot, navigator, bombardier, and me, the tail gunner. We trained in Greenville, North Carolina.

One day I asked the pilot if it would be all right if I took off in the tail. I explained I always took off in the tail of our B-17 in combat.

The pilot said, "No. Not today." I entered the plane and thought, "How's he going to know where I am?" I did not know there was a balance wheel that evened out our weight distribution. So I went to the tail for takeoff.

The pilot taxied to the end of the runway for takeoff. He revved the engines and the plane squatted. He raised the power and revved higher. He then did it again and released the brakes. He was going for a 500-foot takeoff like Jimmy Doolittle on the carrier takeoff for Tokyo in 1942.

At 500 feet down the runway, he lifted the wheels and we dropped just a slight bit. I do not know how our propellers kept from digging up the runway. We got to the end of the runway and there were wires strung across. We went under them then continued contouring the rolling hills for at least a mile or more before gaining enough speed for altitude.

I never told him I took off in the tail and he never asked. I think he scared himself and I know he scared the be-Jesus out of me.

We were slated to finish our training for overseas on August 19, 1945. On the morning of the 15th, I woke up knowing we were just five days from going overseas. For some reason I felt I needed to go to town. I had a class "A" pass and I needed to get away from the confines of the base one last time.

Outside the gate, I picked up a cab and he drove me to town. It was early in the morning and I had no agenda in mind, so I just started to walk the main street.

As I walked by the local bar, I looked over and saw one of my very best friends, an 8th Air Force combat returnee, same as me. He and the bartender were alone and my friend was sloshed.

They invited me in for a drink, but I said it was too early. I suggested to my friend we go back to the base, but he would not have it unless I had a drink with him.

I looked at the bartender, a truly nice person, and he just shrugged and rolled his eyes. On the shelf behind the bar were different size glasses and a pitcher sized one.

I was thinking. Maybe I can get him to pass out with just one more gigantic drink. I stupidly said, "Ok. Since it is just one, let's do the big glass."

I was in a hurry to get him to pass out so we kind of chug-a-lugged. He said, "Just one more, then we'll go."

He was very determined so I reluctantly agreed. As I started the second beer, the first beer caught up to me (no breakfast) and I think I was as inebriated as he was.

Just then, I believe it was 10:00 a.m., sirens sounded, horns tooted and there was a hell of a racket coming from outside.

I stepped out the door and asked a passerby, "What's all the noise about." He said, "Japan has surrendered. The war is over." I looked over my shoulder and both the bartender and my friend were coming out.

My friend was having a hard time navigating, so he leaned up against a lamppost. I said, "Let's grab a cab and get to the base."

My friend said, "Don't want no cab. Just want my own car."

By then, I was so frustrated with him I said, "Look. Here's a truck double-parked on the street with the motor running. Get in and I'll get us back to the base."

My friend was having a hard time standing and, as he was holding on to the post, he started a slow winding slide on the post to the ground. My friend was at least two hundred pounds but a complete docile person. By myself, I could not get him up so two or three fellows helped me and we put him in the passenger seat of the truck.

I went around and got into the driver's seat and put the truck into gear. A policeman directing traffic waved me on through the intersection.

The next street was the main road to our post. I turned right and let the steering wheel loose in my hand so it would turn itself straight.

It did not roll back, but continued across the street. I bumped over a curb into a graveyard fence at about three miles per hour. The engine stalled and I was having trouble restarting the truck.

A second lieutenant came around and asked me to move over, so he could help me out. He started the truck, backed down the street and parked it. He handed me the keys and said he hoped I could handle it from there. I said, "Not my keys. Not my truck." He said, "Oh shit. You and your pal better get out of here.

We all got out of the truck and I helped my friend to a two-foot retaining wall where he sat down and said, "This is my sack. Run, Stevens. I'll take all the blame."

I said, "I'm not leaving you. Let's get a cab and get back to the base." I walked him (half carried him) down the street to where a convertible was parked. I could not stop him; he climbed into the rear seat of the convertible. Again, he said, "This is my sack. Run, Stevens. I'll take the blame."

Just then, four cop cars skidded up and surrounded us. I told him, "Pretend we don't see them. Maybe they'll go away."

They did not and we ended up in the local jail.

We each grabbed a bunk and drifted off to la la land. At about 11:00 p.m. that night, one of the jailers opened the door and said, "The party's over. Go on home."

We took a cab to base, walked through the gate and to our quarters.

That morning, the local papers headlines read, "Two Airmen from the Greenville Air Base Stole a Liquor Truck with $5,000 Worth of Checks and Liquor. They are being held at the base Provost Marshall."

To make a long story short, the Provost Marshall never contacted me or my friend, nor did the local police department. Maybe the bartender spoke up in our behalf, or it was V-J Day (Victory over Japan Day) and the word was "Kings EX (truce). Everyone off free."

I have one word of advice: Do not try to out-drink a drunk. Like my thirty-five missions, I slipped through another crack.

The government did not know exactly what to do with me or any of my combat returnee friends, so they put us in charge of Kitchen Police (KP) and my time schedule was midnight to 7:00 a.m.

Daytime found me in town at the YMCA with a pool and enjoying time at the local pubs.

Come nighttime, as head of KP, we chose steak and eggs and lived the high life. The war was over!! I was mustered out of the service October 1, 1945, and returned home as a civilian.

In the period of time during the war years, all of America was united and we were proud to be Americans. I am still proud to be an American.

HOME AT LAST – AFTER THE WAR

When I returned to civilian life, I went back to work for my father in lathe and plaster.

Since the war was over and soldiers were returning home, women wanted to return to their pre-war status. That is, the women would take care of the home, while the men would take care of earning a living.

My father's secretary gave her notice, so my dad hired a young woman named Henrietta Ochoa as his new secretary. She was just out of high school. In 1950, she became my wife. My father gave us the back half of his lot in Alhambra and I built a small two bedroom home.

My dad retired from his plastering business in 1954, and in 1955, I joined the Alhambra Fire Department.

By 1960, we had five wonderful children, but found our two bedroom home to be too small. We bought a bigger home in a nearby city, Temple City, so as to stay in the area.

Henrietta and I on our wedding day, August 19, 1950

I received my Associate of Arts degree in Fire Science in 1971 and spent the next 18 years as a Fire Captain. I retired with 31 years of fire service in 1986.

In 2012 and 2013, I had the honor and pleasure to visit and ride in the *Aluminum Overcast*" and the Liberty Foundation's *Memphis Belle* (used in the Warner Brothers movie), two of the remaining B-17s as they have been touring the country. I have been fortunate to share with my children and grandchildren the aircraft in which I spent months of my life. It was so important to me that they experience the sights and sounds of the aircraft themselves. I had the opportunity to share my stories and show them the tail position in which I sat for all of my 35 missions.

Me standing in front of the tail position of the *Memphis Belle* in March 2013

Me standing in the mid-section of the plane after returning from a flight around Long Beach, CA on the *Memphis Belle* in March 2013

Me sharing my stories and knowledge with my two youngest grandchildren,
Allison and Roger

Four of my grandchildren with me visiting the *Memphis Belle*
From the left: Allison, Kyle, Me, Stacey, and Roger

The picture below is an image of the tail gunner position on the *Memphis Bell*. In the center is the bicycle seat in which I sat. If I was sitting in the seat, my back would be facing the camera. At the top-center of the picture you can see the view mount (windows). If I pressed my face against the Plexiglas and looked out the windows, I could see up to one o'clock on one side and up to 11 o clock on the other. Just below the window is the area where the machine guns are held. My arms would hug the box and reach inside to grab hold of the machine guns. There is not a lot of room in this position for movement, but I always felt safe and protected.

The tail gunner position on the *Memphis Belle*

An article from the Alhambra Post-Advocate

MEDALS

Most everyone wants to know what we did to earn our medals. Our medals are mostly given as a crew effort rather than for individual heroism. We are like a football team, one man does not get the championship ring. Our trophy comes with delivering our bomb load and getting back alive.

It starts with our pilots getting off the ground with a very heavy bomb and gas load. Then, flying blind through one to two hours of clouds to form our formations as well as the eight to ten hour flight to and from our targets. This also includes flying over the target through the German Fourth of July shoot out equal to a Rose Bowl fireworks display. If you think those German flak gunners scared us, I'm sure our shorts would give a good showing of our bravery. Of course, their fighter planes also added a little spice to the equation.

When our crew was in combat, there was a 1 in 5 or 20 in 100 chance of survival and a 50-50 chance after the 15th mission

Our crew found the crack – after all, **IT ONLY TAKES ONE.**

GUNNER ON FLYING FORTRESS WINS DFC FOR 'ACHIEVEMENT'

AN EIGHTH AIR FORCE BOMBER STATION, England—S/Sgt. Laurence R. Stevens, 20, of Alhambra, Calif., waist gunner on the Eighth Air Force B-17 Flying Fortress "Full House," wears the Distinguished Flying Cross awarded for "extraordinary achievement"

LAURENCE R. STEVENS

while participating in more than a score of heavy bombing assaults on vital Nazi targets in Europe and in support of advances by the ground troops in France. The presentation was made by Col. Karl Truesdell jr., of Washington, D. C., a group commander in the 3rd Bombardment Division, which was cited by the President for its now historic England-Africa shuttle bombing of Messerschmitt aircraft plants in Regensburg, Germany, last summer.

Sgt. Stevens, already holder of the Air Medal with four Oak Leaf Clusters, is the son of Mr. and Mrs. Tony A. Stevens, 1102 South Edith Avenue, Alhambra. Before his entrance in the service in April, 1943, he was a student at Alhambra High School, where he was captain on the Moor football team.

An older brother Sgt. Ernest Stevens, U. S. Army, was reported last November as killed in action while serving in Italy. Another brother, James, is serving in the Merchant Marine somewhere overseas.

An article from the Alhambra Post-Advocate

Oak Leaf Cluster to AM
GENERAL ORDERS)

RESTRICTED

Hq 3d Bombardment Division
APO 559

NO.   203)

EXTRACT

14 June   1944

Under the provisions of Army Regulations 600-45, 22 September 1943, and pursuant to authority contained in ltr 200.6, Hq. Eighth Air Force, 2 April 1944, subject: "Awards and Decorations," an OAK LEAF CLUSTER is awarded, for wear with the Air Medal previously awarded, to the following-named Enlisted Man, organization as indicated, Army Air Forces, United States Army.

Citation: For exceptionally meritorious achievement, while participating in heavy bombardment missions over enemy occupied Continental Europe. The courage, coolness and skill displayed by this Enlisted Man upon these occasions reflects great credit upon himself and the Armed Forces of the United States.

*   *   *

LAURENCE R. STEVENS, 39570296, Sergeant, 412th Bombardment Squadron (H)
                                    95th Bombardment Group (H)
                                              *   *

By command of Major General LE MAY:

OFFICIAL:

O. T. DRAEWELL
Major, Air Corps
Adjutant General

A. W. KISSNER
Brigadier General, USA
Chief of Staff

RESTRICTED

77

TABLE OF MISSIONS

MISSION #	DATE	TAKEOFF TIME	TIME LOGGED	TARGET
1	Tuesday, April 25, 1944	6:00 a.m.	8 hrs 45 mins	Dijon, France
2	Wednesday, April 26, 1944	6:30 a.m.	7 hrs 40 mins	Brunswick, Germany
3	Thursday, April 27, 1944	6:00 a.m.	5 hrs 30 mins	Flottemanville-Hague, Cherbourg
4	Thursday, April 27, 1944	Afternoon takeoff	6 hrs 15 mins (11 hr 45 mins for day)	Le Culot, France
5	Friday, April 28, 1944	7:30 a.m. (Went to bed at midnight)	5 hrs	Sottevast, Cherbourg, military installations
6	Saturday, April 29, 1944	6:30 a.m.	9 hrs 15 mins	Berlin, Germany
7	Monday, May 1, 1944	Late takeoff, 2:30 p.m.	7 hrs	Berlin, Germany. Sarreguemines, France, marshalling yards (train depots).

PLANE/ SERIAL NUMBER	GROUP POSITION	OPPOSITION
Fireball / 231876	Tail-Ass Charlie	Light flak, no enemy fighters
Full House, B-17 G 297797	Element Lead	No fighter attacks but considerable flak on the bomb run.
Full House	Tail-Ass Charlie	Coastal bombing. Flak was precise and heavy. Goofed and flew under entire formation while on bomb run.
Full House	Tail-Ass Charlie	Targets A and B were heavily overcast. Bombed target C and we were credited with good bombing.
Full House	Purple Heart Corner	Flak so intense over target, it broke up formation resulting in a dry run. Almost went back but decided it was suicide, so called it a day. We were credited for a mission.
Knock Out Baby (also known as "Armored Baby")	Wingman	Meager flak to the target; intense flak over Berlin, Brunswick and Hanover (which we were warned to miss).
Full House	Wingman	Encountered approximately seven ME 109s. Got off a short burst of a few hundred rounds. Not nervous, just ready.

MISSION #	DATE	TAKEOFF TIME	TIME LOGGED	TARGET
8 (Scrubbed)	Thursday, May 4, 1944			Berlin
8	Monday, May 8, 1944	6:00 a.m.	8 hrs 20 mins	Berlin
9	Tuesday, May 9, 1944	6:10 a.m.	5 hrs 20 mins	Laon, France
10 (Scrubbed)	Wednesday, May 10, 1944	5:30 a.m.		Fallersleben, Germany
10	Thursday, May 11, 1944	2:55 p.m.	5 hrs 30 mins	Liège, Belgium, marshalling yards
11	Friday, May 12, 1944		9 hrs 30 mins	Brux, Czechoslovakia, oil field
12	Friday, May 19, 1944	9:00 a.m.	9 hrs 35 mins	Berlin

PLANE/ SERIAL NUMBER	GROUP POSITION	OPPOSITION
Full House		Scrubbed after takeoff because of weather.
Full House		Seemed as though all flak guns trained on us as flak literally blanketed the skies.
Full House		Intense flak. No fighters.
Full House		Intense fog. Flew through a whole formation of aircrafts, narrowly missing on another. Mission was scrubbed and we found our way back to base.
Full House		Intense flak.
Full House		Intense fighter activity. Two bomb runs over target.
Full House		Fighter activity. Heavy flak.

MISSION #	DATE	TAKEOFF TIME	TIME LOGGED	TARGET
13	Thursday, May 25, 1944	4:56 a.m.	5 hrs 45 mins	Brussels, Belgium, marshalling yards
14	Tuesday, May 30, 1944	7:15 a.m.	4 hrs 30 mins	Brussels, Belgium, again, marshalling yards
15	Friday, June 2, 1944	9:00 a.m.	4 hrs 23 mins	"No Ball" France, coastal bomb installations or V1 or V2 rocket launching sites.
16	Tuesday, June 6, 1944 (D-Day)	7:00 a.m.	5 hrs	Normandy, France
17	Wednesday, June 7, 1944 (Day after D-Day)	3:35 p.m.	7 hrs 30 mins	Nantes, France
18 (Scrubbed)	Saturday, June 10, 1944			An airfield in France
18	Monday, June 12, 1944	4:35 a.m.	6 hrs	An airfield in France.

PLANE/ SERIAL NUMBER	GROUP POSITION	OPPOSITION
Full House		No fighters. Meager flak.
Full House		No fighters. Tracking flak.
Full House		.Rocket type missiles
Taint a Bird II, #1989, F model	Middle group	We missed the entire D-Day invasion. The day was so overcast that we did not drop our bombs but returned them to our base. Our mission did count even though we did not drop our bombs. Germany did not put up a single plane. The skies belonged to us.
Full House	Second element lead in lead squadron	Today we had better weather and we saw the invasion fleet and the invasion coast from 21,000 feet; however, we were too high to see any of the ground battles.
Full House		Our rendezvous was to be at 21,000 feet, but weather so bad, we ended up at an altitude of 27,000 feet. Vapor trails and clouds finally caused us to scrub the mission.
Full House	High squadron lead	Original target overcast. Toured the whole of France and gave the Ack Ack gunners plenty of target practice.

MISSION #	DATE	TAKEOFF TIME	TIME LOGGED	TARGET
19	Wednesday, June 14, 1944	3:55 a.m.	6 hrs 45 mins	St. Trond, Belgium, airfield, overcast. Airfield in Chièvres, France.
20	Sunday, June 18, 1944	5:20 a.m.	6 hrs 30 mins	Hanover, Germany
21	Friday, June 23, 1944	3:00 p.m.	5 hrs 45 mins	Paris, France
22	Thursday, June 29, 1944	4:00 a.m.	8 hrs	Leipzig, Böhlen
23	Friday, July 7, 1944	5:10 a.m.	6 hrs 50 mins	Kölleda, Germany
24	Tuesday, July 11, 1944	8:30 a.m.	9 hrs 5 mins	Munich, Germany
Note	Tuesday, July 11, 1944			
25	Wednesday, July 12, 1944	8:30 a.m.	9 hrs	Munich, Germany, Focke-Wulf assembly plant

PLANE/ SERIAL NUMBER	GROUP POSITION	OPPOSITION
Full House	Low squadron lead	After bombs away, we discovered half our bomb load was still hung up, so we left the formation and salvoed them in the Channel. Landed a half hour late to find ground crew sweating us out. Lost one 412 ship. Wells, the pilot from our training group from Avon Park, Florida.
Full House	Low squadron lead	Heavy flak, no fighters. When we hit the IP (Initial Point which is the start of a bomb run), the clouds were so heavy over and under us that we lost track of the other squadrons and dropped our bombs early.
Full House	Low squadron lead	Heavy flak. Behind us got a direct hit and nosed straight down. No survivors. All ships of our group returned with flak damage. Flak was the heaviest I had ever seen.
Full House	Low squadron lead	Made three runs on a clear day and not once did we ever get out of their flak range. Seven ME109's made one pass.
Ready Freddy	Low squadron lead	Intensive tracking flak. Made dry runs over primary and secondary targets, bombing of Kölleda, Germany was termed excellent.
Full House	Low squadron lead	Had hangover from polishing off a fifth of Scotch for my birthday, July 10th. Lost one engine to flak. Saw ship of my California buddy, Snake Carpenter, get a direct hit by flak. Thought for sure they were goners. Snake was wounded and sent home.
		Missions upped from 25 to 30.
Full House	Low squadron lead	Encountered heavy flak over the target. Germans reported we were dropping a lot of "duds." Unknown to them, these were timed bombs to go off at a later hour. Such is war.

MISSION #	DATE	TAKEOFF TIME	TIME LOGGED	TARGET
26	Sunday, July 16, 1944	5:30 a.m.	8 hrs	Stuttgart, Germany
27	Tuesday, July 18, 1944	4:45 a.m.	6 hrs 30 mins	Hemmingstedt, Germany, oil storage tanks
28	Thursday, July 20, 1944	6:30 a.m.	8 hrs 30 mins	Lutzkendorf, Germany, (Leipzig) oil storage tanks.
29	Tuesday, August 1, 1944	10:20 a.m.	9 hrs 20 mins	Cadillac, France, air drops to the French Marquis.
Note	Wednesday, August 2, 1944			
30	Thursday, August 3, 1944	12:10 p.m.	5 hrs 30 mins	Bridge in France
31	Sunday, August 6, 1944		9 hrs 45 mins	Airdrome at Rahmel (Gdynia) in the Polish Corridor.

PLANE/ SERIAL NUMBER	GROUP POSITION	OPPOSITION
Full House	Low squadron lead	Primary target, overcast. Bombed secondary target, Stuttgart, Germany. Bombing results were unknown.
Full House	High squadron lead	Target completely overcast, so we bombed by PFF (Path Finder, a new method of bombing through clouds by radar). Results: Unknown.
Full House	High squadron lead	Heavy flak. No fighters. Target again overcast. Bombed by PFF (Path Finder). Waist gunner Rogers was taken off our crew. Now a 9 man crew.
Full House	High squadron lead	Dropped care package to free French marquis at the top of the Swiss Alps. Heated suit burnt out. I froze.
		Missions upped from 30 to 35.
Full House	High squadron lead	Caught some flak over Caen and came home without dropping our bombs. The mission counted because we were in enemy territory and encountered flak.
Full House	High squadron lead	Our bombing called "good." First leg of shuttle run to Poltava, Russia. Seven P97's plainly marked with German swastikas flew near and directly over us with no shots fired.

MISSION #	DATE	TAKEOFF TIME	TIME LOGGED	TARGET
32	Monday, August 7, 1944	6:00 a.m.	10 hrs	Trzebinia, Poland, oil refinery Shuttle run
33	Tuesday, August 8, 1944		8 hrs 30 mins	Buzău, Romania Shuttle run
34	Saturday, August 12, 1944		9 hrs 15 mins	Toulouse, France airfield Shuttle run
Note	Tuesday, August 15, 1944			Zeitz, Germany
35	Friday, August 25, 1944			Politz, Austria
Note				

PLANE/ SERIAL NUMBER	GROUP POSITION	OPPOSITION
Full House	High squadron lead	Mission out of Poltava, Russia. Fire at base of upper turret. Navigator Morrison and Bombardier Sherwood bailed out over Russia.
Full House	High squadron lead	We were told our bombing was good. Entire mission overcast. Never saw the ground, only mountain tops.
Full House	High squadron lead	Milk run.
Full House		*Full House* with new crew, first mission shot down over Zeitz, Germany by a 105 flak gun. Took another B-17 down with them
Big Chief Illiniwek B-17 G – New plane, first mission	High squadron lead	For the first time on our tour, we had to abort. We turned and headed home alone. I would like to claim five enemy German seagulls. I shot them down over the English Channel.
		35 missions successfully completed.

Made in the USA
Middletown, DE
17 March 2025

72768153R00059